The
Philosophy
of
Social Ecology

Essays on Dialectical Naturalism

Murray Bookchin

**BLACK
ROSE
BOOKS**

Montréal/New York
London

BLACK ROSE BOOKS No. Y225
Hardcover ISBN 1-551640-19-8
Paperback ISBN 1-551640-18-X

Canadian Cataloguing in Publication Data

Bookchin, Murray, 1921
The philosophy of social ecology: essays on dialectical naturalism

2nd ed., rev.
ISBN 1-551649-19-8 (bound)
ISBN 1-551640-18-X (pbk.)

1. Human ecology. I. Title
HM206.B65 1995 304.2 C95-900141-7

Mailing Address

BLACK ROSE BOOKS
C.P. 1258
Succ. Place du Parc
Montréal, Québec
H2W 2R3 Canada

BLACK ROSE BOOKS
340 Nagel Drive
Cheektowaga, New York
14225 USA

Printed in Canada on acid-free paper

A publication of the Institute of Policy Alternatives of Montréal
(IPAM)

CONTENTS

For Janet Biehl,
dearest of companions and closest of colleagues

Preface to the Second Edition

This edition of *The Philosophy of Social Ecology* has been so radically revised and corrected that in many respects it is a new book. I have retained in most of their essentials the essays that appeared in the first edition, but I have significantly altered many of my original formulations. I have also added a new essay, "History, Civilization, and Progress," written early in 1994, which critically examines in general terms the social and ethical relativism so much in vogue today.

Most of the essays in this book were written as polemics, directed against various tendencies that surfaced in the American ecology movement in the 1980s. "Toward a Philosophy of Nature," published in Michael Tobias's misnamed collection, *Deep Ecology*, in

1985 but written three years earlier for the journal *Telos,* was directed against the then-current enthusiasm for turning systems theory into ecological philosophy. "Freedom and Necessity in Nature," published in the Canadian journal *Alternatives* in 1986, challenged the neo-Darwinian view of the natural world fostered by a cluster of very conventional ecologists and initiated my critique of "biocentrism." "Thinking Ecologically," initially published in 1987 in another Canadian journal, *Our Generation,* was written to criticize the New Age "paradigm" that was then being inflicted on the ecology movement, as well as certain leaders of Earth First!, who were then advancing a crudely misanthropic message from their stronghold in the American Sunbelt. Appearing here in the order in which they were written (except for the introduction), they are thus set in very distinct time frames, with emphases appropriate to issues that have emerged over the past fourteen years. I wish to thank all previous publishers of these essays for their permission to republish them, both in the original and in this revised edition.

Although times have changed since these essays first appeared, the problems they tried to address are still with us. Gregory Bateson's views no longer enjoy the preeminence that they did in the 1980s, for example, but his subjectivism and many of his arguments played a major role in forming the innerworldly, relativistic, and personalistic Zeitgeist of present New Age ideologues, while systems theory approaches still surface in many current theoretical works on ecology. Fritjof Capra is still fostering his eclectic medley of science and mysticism, of Prigoginian systems theory and "California cosmology." "Biocentrism," antihumanism, deep ecology, and neo-Malthusianism have become even more popular than they were when I wrote "Thinking Ecologically." New views have melded with older ones: today, it is philosophical relativism and postmodernism that are percolating through the ecology movement; hence the new closing essay, "History, Civilization, and Progress." In revising all the essays, I have tried to generalize the views expressed in the original versions to make them as relevant as possible to present-day discussion. Let me add that without the assistance and editorial insights of Janet Biehl, to whom this book is dedicated, these revisions would have been difficult to make. I would also like to express my thanks to Nathalie Klym at Black Rose Books for her valuable work in producing this book.

Two other changes in the present edition should be singled out. First, I have excised favorable references to the Frankfurt School and Theodor Adorno. Like Leszek Kolakowski, I have come to regard much of Adorno's work as intellectually irresponsible, wayward, and poorly theorized, despite the brilliance of his style (at times) and his often insightful epigrams. This is not to reject his defense of speculative reason against positivism—which was what initially attracted me to his work and to the Frankfurt School—even as his writings exude enormous pessimism about reason and its destiny.

Second, I have removed my favorable allusions to ideas that have since become central to ecofeminism. The exciting challenge that radical feminism posed in the early 1970s was its universal condemnation of hierarchy as such, which appealed to me since I myself had made such a condemnation more than a decade earlier. Even in the late 1970s, when ecofeminism emerged, claims of the "innate" superiority of females over males and of women's superior emotional and cognitive abilities, and opposition to "logocentrism," were not yet prominent. Only later was ecofeminism reduced to the antirational and crudely visceral level of a Starhawk, where invocations of magic, goddess worship, and witchcraft become "feminist" ways of eluding reality. Too many ecofeminists, albeit not all, now tend to privilege women over men cognitively and morally, while the original universalist and egalitarian approach of the feminist movement has withered significantly.

Whether the reader agrees with all my views or not, these essays, I believe, are required reading for anyone who wishes to understand social ecology. They seek, more suggestively than exhaustively, to establish its philosophical foundations and modes of thought. (Let me insist that they are the works of neither a "Hegelian," a "neo-Hegelian," nor a "post-Hegelian," to use current academic jargon, but rather of a *dialectician* upon whom Hegel exercised a considerable influence.) A rounded understanding of social ecology as I have formulated it, however, also requires a reading of at least two of my other books, *Remaking Society* and *Urbanization Without Cities*, which explore social ecology's historical and political aspects.

Recent developments in quasi-leftist social thinking have obliged me to significantly alter the way I conceive *nature, society,* and *reason,* as well as *history, civilization,* and *progress,* as the reader will find in the closing essay. All these words have a multiplicity of meanings, but the meanings that are most pervasive today are not the ones that I intend when I use these words. Nowadays, for example, the ecology movement most often regards *nature* either as a "social construction" or a "wilderness" of one sort or another, while others see *society* as *any* aggregation of life-forms, including flocks of birds and herds of deer. Both within and without the ecology movement, *reason* is regarded as a mental skill, *history* as a mere succession of events, *civilization* as a

Eurocentri c prejudice, and *progress* as a myth. Years of give-and-take with both supporters and opponents of my views have obliged me to slowly but consciously give these words a more specific philosophical meaning than they have in conventional discourse. Some of these changes are discussed in the new introduction to the Black Rose edition of *The Ecology of Freedom;* others require elucidation here.

As I explain in the introduction to this book, *Nature* properly encompasses everything around us, from the organic beings that we normally designate as "natural" to the lifeless moon that appears on relatively cloudless nights—that is, the totality of Being. However, if we are to use the word *Nature* in any more specific sense, we should use an adjective before it, to describe what *aspect* of "nature" we are talking about—something that I often did not do in these essays, owing to the time period in which they were written. The reader who encounters the word *nature* herein, unmodified by any adjective, should now take it to refer to my notion of "first nature," or the cumulative evolution of the natural world, especially the organic world. This first nature exists in both continuity *and* discontinuity with "second nature," or the evolution of society. As I discuss in some detail in "Thinking Ecologically," second nature develops both in continuity with first nature and as its antithesis, until the two are sublated into "free nature" or "Nature" rendered self-conscious in a rational and ecological society.

Society, in turn, is more than mere consociation or community. It is *institutionalized* community, structured around mutable organizational forms that may range from totalitarian despotism to libertarian municipalism. As such, society is specific to human beings; indeed, an expression like "social insects" is, from my standpoint, nonsensical and oxymoronic, conflating a fixed, genetically programmed aggregation of animals with the developmentally structured consociation of humans. As for *reason* and *rationality,* when I use these terms without any qualifying adjective, I mean *dialectical reason,* a secular dialectical *logos,* as contrasted with *instrumental* or *conventional reason,* an ordinary mental skill. *History,* as I argue in the final essay, is the cultural and social unfolding of reason, not simply a succession of events over time, for which I reserve the word *Chronicles. Civilization* is the actualization in varying degrees of historical unfolding, while *Progress* is, more loosely, the self-directive activity of History and Civilization toward increasing rationality, freedom, and self-consciousness in relationships between human and human, and in the relationship of humanity to the natural world.

Let me state as clearly and firmly as possible that I do not regard History and Progress as unilinear, inevitable, teleological, or in any sense predetermined. The power of speculative reason to logically project beyond the given into what is yet to come *if* humanity acts rationally—a power that is one of our highest *human* attributes—does not mean that what rationally "should be" will indeed *necessarily* "be." To constitute the all-important standard by which we may judge the rationality of a society is a firmly held function of dialectical reason. We would lose ourselves in a quagmire of solipsistic relativism if we were to abdicate the power of reason to "judge" History, Civilization, and Progress. Even the most dyed-in-the-wool antirationalists and relativists exercise this power, irrespective of their convictions against doing so. As any thinking person would agree, people do indeed imagine the world as it *might* be, in contrast to what it *is* in reality, even in their daydreams. They do have the wildest fantasies about their culture and its environment. And they do hold the most seemingly un-realistic constellations of images and "patterns of culture" about basic aspects of their experience. None of this do I deny—quite the contrary, humanity's continual *struggle* with its imagination lies at the very heart of the tensions within early society, which in turn has historically led to varying degrees of rational self-under-standing as well as frightening, often atavistic regressions.

Given these observations, it would be simplistic and one-sided to ignore the moral and cultural paradoxes embedded in so-cial development. Humanity did not emerge *ab novo,* without roots in animal evolution. The human being has been and still is an animal with emotional states that are animalistic, like "fight and flight" reactions and tormentingly basic fears. But humans are also animals of a very special kind: we are highly intelligent by com-parison with other species—indeed, qualitatively so—and as such, we have the ability not only to adapt to our environments but intentionally to alter them significantly. In short, we can do more than adapt; we can *innovate,* although we do not always innovate willingly if we can survive in a given environment without doing so.

Our intelligence is also highly problematic. It makes not only for innovation but for foresight, fantasy, imagination, creativity—and cruelty. Indeed, much personal and social ir-rationality *stems* from the intentionality, will, self-assertiveness, and fantasies of our animality informed by our intelligence. As Marx suggested, we still live in prehistory and have yet to find our way toward a self-conscious, humane, cooperative, and empathetic so-cial life. With our animalistic as well as human attributes, we evolve in an ever-changing world and face stark problems of sur-vival and well-being. Apart from those people who inhabit places with benign physiographic conditions, we are subject to material insecurity, contesting wills, challenges to our sense of self and self-regard, fears of disease, diminishing physical powers with age, frightening dreams, and so forth. We address these abiding problems with relatively developed minds that are still encased, as it were, in extremely potent animal attributes.

History is the painful movement of human beings in extricating themselves from animal existence, of the emergence of tensions from a combination of nonhuman and human attributes, and of progressively advancing toward a more universally human state of affairs, however irregular or unsteady this advance may be. The problems that humans retain from early society continue to exist in one way or another to this day, and their resolution in part or whole is one of the meaningful goals of History, even as new problems arise over the course of time. Nor is there any certainty that these problems will be resolved. A descent into barbarism—a problematic that Marxists were raising during the grimmest years of World War II—is just as possible as the attainment of a rational society.

But to deny, because of such starkly conflicting alternatives in social development, that there are rational criteria by which we may judge that Progress is myopic, or even that Progress has occurred, is self-deceptive. It is all too easy to rebuke History if one minimizes the genuine advances that have been made in culture, social relations, and technics. All doubts about History, Civilization, and Progress aside, it is undeniable that we have divested ourselves of many of the kinship ties that parochialized us into tribal groups, and that we have accepted—albeit with many qualifications—our status as a *human* species rather than as a *folk*. We have created cities that are open to strangers, we have advanced technology to the point that a sufficiency in the means of life could be available to all in a rational society, and we have increased our knowledge of the natural world to almost sublime proportions. Not only do we kill each other with terrifying brutality, given our combination of animality with intelligence, but we help each other on a massive scale with extraordinary sensitivity.

Here, I believe, we are obliged to make a serious decision about how we look at the past. Either we will relativize History by emphasizing the power of the irrational over human behavior and the endless differences that distinguish cultures from one another; or we will emphasize the remarkable coherence of various cultures and generalize from their similarities, even as we appreciate their differences. Choosing the first alternative would ultimately diminish social development to a disconnected archipelago of wholly unique cultures whose only coherence is psychosocial and internal; while the second alternative would allow for a dialectically rational understanding of History and a ground for ethics. If our animalistic *capacity* for irrational behavior gains priority over our humanistic *potentiality* to act rationally, and if social development becomes only an ensemble of *Chronicles* (if even that) rather than a *History* of maturation, there is no basis for striving to achieve a rational society.

What, then, of those social failures, aberrations, horrors, and breakdowns that belie humanity's unilinear progress toward Civilization and freedom?[1] Without in any way *understating* this problematic, we must be wary of *overstating* it by dissolving social development in psychosocial interpretations, thereby minimizing the very reality of social maturation as such. There has been a historical social development, all its many setbacks notwithstanding, setbacks that can in part be attributed to elites of agonistic men whose power gave them the scope to play out their destructive fantasies, impulses, and designs on a large social stage. In their activities they have "gone too far," so to speak, demonically pushing cultures beyond the rational framework of their historical time. Such distortions become especially problematical during times of transition, when established social formations are being negated and new ones are emerging with uncertainty and ambiguity. This overextension of the "negative" (to use Hegel's term) occurred at numerous times and in numerous places, when "antitheses" became ends in themselves and did not develop as a rational or progressive transcendence. Neither tribal, feudal, autocratic, republican, nor even classical democratic political systems have been historically immune to this phenomenon.

And yet it would be a gross simplification of social development to ahistorically dichotomize the hierarchical, class, and even state formations of the past, on the one hand, and the torturous efforts of humanity to advance toward freedom, on the other. Paradoxically, in its emergence out of barbarism—indeed, out of simple animality—humanity may have had to depend upon priests, chieftains, and perhaps state-like formations to overcome parochialism, lack of individuality, kinship bonds, gerontocracies, and patriarchies, to cite some key social features of tribal and even civilized cultures. "Evils" these are, to be sure, but, if we are to believe Michael Bakunin, "socially necessary evils," a phrase with which he historically characterized the state and that Peter Kropotkin echoed in his famous *Encyclopaedia Britannica* article, "Anarchism." The groundwork for making a civilizatory process possible—notably the emergence of cities, territorial forms of consociation, writing, an expanding moral sensibility, a rational and incipiently secular outlook on the world, technological advances that led to agriculture, metallurgy, and relatively sophisticated crafts—all may have required what we would regard today as unacceptable institutions of social control but that at an earlier time may have been important in launching a rational social development.

In any case, to ahistorically counterpose "virtue" to "evil" without *any* historical qualifications and mediations can be very naïve. In much earlier historical eras, "good" and "evil" had not even acquired the *definitions* they have today, after thousands of years of human social development. The state's invasion of patriarchal authority; its substitution of a relatively rational system of law for the patriarch's arbitrary and absolute authority over all other members of a family or clan; and the abrogation of blood vengeance as a way of resolving conflicts—all, to cite some significant advances, played a role that was relatively liberatory in its historical context, given a general framework of domination in early hierarchical societies. Patriarchs, for example, would have seen the state's function in this respect as "evil."

Like the historical replacement of kinship ties with civic ties, barter with markets, agrarian isolation with cities, particularism with growing universalism, and superstition with secularism, there were certain forms of socially regulative institutions that, while oppressive in modern eyes, opened possibilities for liberatory developments that otherwise might never have emerged. But although the very real barbarism of past and present remains an "evil," as Bakunin observed, it was not a historical "necessity" in any sense akin to Bakunin's, for we can never know what rational alternatives may have existed at any time. At no time can we surrender to the "inevitability" of domination in certainty that latent liberatory possibilities do not exist.

In no sense, then, should my remarks be seen as an "excuse" for barbaric behavior, past or present. Rather, I intend them in great part to be the premise for trying to *understand* how it is that the irrational dimensions of the past, with their many barbarities, never completely stifled the rational development of humanity and yet may have even interacted with it at times to yield social advances within a broadly evil framework. It behooves us to study the historical and social *interactions* between the legacy of freedom and the legacy of domination, in degree as well as in kind, not to simplify them or even brush them aside with psychosocial categories or ahistorically enumerate them on a social ledger of debits and credits. If we are to think in a graded and nuanced manner, with a modicum of intellectual responsibility, about the past and present, we are obliged to explore the social conditions in which—offensive as it may seem to "politically correct" modern minds—certain forms of domination paradoxically provided the stimulus for increasing freedom, culturally if not institutionally.

Do we have no other ground than our personal preferences for dealing with the social issues of the past and present? Attitudes, wishes, desires, and imagined ways of life are deeply rooted in existing social conditions—not even our most liberating "preferences" have solely personal origins. Today they reflect possibilities and hopes that were not available to the radical culture of only a few generations ago. The cry to "demand the impossible," which surfaced among French students in May-June 1968, rested massively on the extraordinary *possibilities* that advances in technology and material life had opened up, not simply on aliena-tion—which, in fact, these very advances significantly generated.

The essays in this book critique the common view that—owing to the "impossibility" of formulating an objective criterion for determining what is rational or irrational, real or imaginary, true or false, good or evil, self-determining or authoritarian—our attitude that freedom is desirable and tyranny hateful must have only a contingent subjective basis. When this attitude is formed *in abstracto,* without any roots in historical development or material preconditions, it remains theoretically unjustified and a mere mat-ter of opinion. Unfortunately, this is an indulgence we can ill af-ford. The condition of the world is far too desperate and chaotic for us, often from the fastness of the academy, to advance a moral, social, and cultural incoherence that rests primarily on attitudes, tastes, and matters of opinion that themselves beg for rational ex-planation.

—March 15, 1994

NOTE

1. The notion of a unilinear social development, like the one Friedrich Engels presented in *Anti-Dühring*, had already fallen into considerable disrepute among serious Marxists in the first half of this century, as I myself recall. One of the most troubling problems with this notion, I should note, was the "transition" from feudalism to capitalism. For my own part, I clearly challenged the idea that capitalism was the "inevitable" successor of feudalism in *Urbanization Without Cities*. There I argued that capitalism, from the fourteenth century until well into the eighteenth and early nineteenth, was merely *part* of "a mixed economy which was neither feudal, capitalist, nor structured around simple commodity production. Rather, it contained and combined elements of all three forms." Economically as well as culturally, an open situation, so to speak, existed that could quite conceivably have led to more benign social advances and avoided the horrors that capitalism brought into the world. See *Urbanization Without Cities* (originally published as *The Rise of Urbanization and the Decline of Citizenship* by Sierra Club Books in 1987; published in Canada by Montreal: Black Rose Books, 1992), pp. 198-201. In this book I consistently emphasize the significance of libertarian municipalist confederations in opposition to the state—historically as well as contemporaneously.

INTRODUCTION
A Philosophical Naturalism

What is nature? What is humanity's place in nature? And what is the relationship of society to the natural world?

In an era of ecological breakdown, answering these questions has become of momentous importance for our everyday lives and for the future that we and other life-forms face. They are not abstract philosophical questions that should be relegated to a remote, airy world of metaphysical speculation. Nor can we answer them in an offhand way, with poetic metaphors or unthinking, visceral reactions. The definitions and ethical standards with which we respond to them may ultimately decide whether human society will creatively foster natural evolution, or whether we will render the planet uninhabitable for all complex life-forms, including ourselves.

At first glance, everybody "knows" what nature is. It is that which is all around us—trees, animals, rocks, and the like. It is that which "humanity" is coating with petroleum or destroying. But such prima facie definitions fall apart when we examine them with some care. If nature is indeed what is all around us, we may reasonably ask, then, is a carefully manicured suburban lawn not nature? Is the split-level house it surrounds not nature? Are its furnishings not natural?

Today, this sort of question is likely to elicit a heated avowal that only "wild," "primordial," or even nonhuman nature is authentically natural. Other people, no less thoughtful, will reply that nature is basically matter, or the materialized stuff of the universe in all its forms—what philosophers sweepingly call *Being*. The fact is that wide philosophical differences have existed for centuries in the West over the very definition of the word *nature*. These differences remain unresolved to this day, even as nature is making headlines in environmental issues that are of enormous importance for the future of nearly all life-forms.

Defining *nature* becomes an even more complex task when we include the human species as part of it. Is human society with its ensemble of technologies and artifacts—not to speak of such ineffable features as its conflicting social interests and institutions—any less part of nature than nonhuman animals? And if human beings are part of nature, are they merely one life-form among many others, or are they unique in ways that place major responsibilities on them with respect to the rest of the world of life, responsibilities that no other species shares or is even capable of sharing?

Whatever *nature* may mean, we must determine in what way humanity "fits" into it. And we must confront the complex and challenging question of the relationship of society—more specifically, the different social forms that appeared in the past, that exist today, and that may appear in the future—to nature. Unless we answer these questions with reasonable clarity—or at least fully discuss them—we will lack any ethical direction in dealing with our environmental problems. Unless we know what nature is and what humanity's and society's place in it is, we will be left with vague intuitions and visceral sentiments that neither cohere into clear views nor provide a guide for effective action.

*

It is easy to try to escape answering these troubling questions by impatiently rejecting them, responding with pure emotion, or simply denigrating any effort to reason out a coherent reply— indeed, by attacking reason *itself* as "meddlesome" (to use William Blake's term). Today, even sensitive people in growing numbers feel betrayed by the centuries-long glorification of reason, with its icy claims to efficiency, objectivity, and freedom from ethical constraint—or the form of reason that has nourished particularly destructive technologies like nucleonics and weaponry. This negative popular reaction is understandable. But swerving away from a specific form of reason that is largely instrumental and coldly analytical creates problems that are no less disturbing than those questions from which we are seeking to escape.

In our aversion to an insensitive and unfeeling form of reason, we may easily opt for a cloudy intuitionism and mysticism as an alternative. Unlike instrumental and analytical reason, after all, a surrender to emotion and mythic beliefs yields cooperative feelings of "interconnectedness" with the natural world and perhaps even a caring attitude toward it. But precisely because intuition and mystical beliefs are so cloudy and arbitrary—which is to say, so *un*reasoned—they may also "connect" us with things we really shouldn't be connected with at all—namely, racism, sexism, and an abject subservience to charismatic leaders.

Indeed, following this intuitional alternative could potentially render our ecological outlook very dangerous. Vital as the idea of "interconnectedness" may be to our views, it has historically often been the basis of myths and supernatural beliefs that became means for social control and political manipulation. The first half of the twentieth century is in great part the story of brutal movements like National Socialism that fed on a popular antirationalism and anti-intellectualism, and a personal sense of alienation, among other things. This movement mobilized and homogenized millions of people with an antisocial, perverted "ecologistic" ideology based on intuition, with an "interconnectedness" of earth, folk, and "blood and soil" that was militaristic and murderous rather than freely communitarian. Insulated from the challenge of rational critique by its anti-intellectualism and mythic nationalism, the National Socialist movement eventually turned much of Europe into a cemetery. Yet ideologically, this fascist totalitarianism had gained sustenance from the intuitional and mystical credo of the Romantic movement of the century before—something no one could have foreseen at the time.

Feeling, sentiment, and a moral outlook we surely need if instrumental and analytical reason are not to divest us of our *pas-*

sion for truth. But myths, mind-numbing rituals, and charismatic personalities can also rob us of the critical faculties that thought provides. Recently, a Green organization in Canada flippantly proclaimed that it seeks "cooperation" as part of its "new paradigm" rather than "confrontation," which it considers part of the rejected "old paradigm." In a more radical era, confrontation was the stated purpose of radical movements! The mythic and uncritical aspect of "interconnectedness" that rejects confrontation seems to have reduced this Canadian Green organization to the level of outright accommodation with the status quo. Here, the need not only to confront the evils of our time but to uncompromisingly oppose them has disappeared into a New Age quagmire of unthinking "good vibes." The "loving" path of compromises along which such "good vibes" leads us can easily end in sheer opportunism.

If our contemporary revolt against reason rests on the misguided belief that the only alternative to our present reality is mysticism, it also rests on the equally misguided belief that only one kind of reason exists. In reacting against instrumental and analytical forms of reason, which are usually identified with reason as such, we may well overlook *other forms of reason* that are organic and yet retain critical qualities; that are developmental and yet retain analytical insights; that are ethical and yet retain contact with reality. The "value-free" rationalism that we normally identify with the physical sciences and technology is in fact not the only form of reason that Western philosophy has developed over the centuries—I refer specifically to the great tradition of dialectical reason that originated in Greece some twenty-five centuries ago and reached its high point, but by no means its completion, in the logical works of Hegel.

What dialectical thinkers from Heraclitus onward have had in common, in varying degrees, is a view of reality as developmental—of *Being* as an ever-unfolding *Becoming*. Ever since Plato created a dualism between a supranatural world of ideal forms and a transient world of imperfect sensible copies, the perplexing question of identity amid change and change amid identity has haunted Western philosophy. Instrumental and analytical forms of reason—what I will here generically call *conventional reason*[1]—rest on a fundamental principle, the famous "principle of identity," or *A equals A,* which means that any given phenomenon can be only itself and cannot be other than what it is, or what we immediately perceive it to be, at a given moment in time. Without this principle, logical consistency in conventional reason would be impossible.

Conventional reason is based on an analysis of phenomena as precisely defined, and whose truth depends upon their internal consistency and practicality. It focuses on a thing or phenomenon as fixed, with clear-cut boundaries that are immutable for analytical purposes. We know an entity, in this widely accepted notion of reason, when we can analyze it into its irreducible components and determine how they work as a functioning whole so that knowledge of the entity will have operational applicability. When the boundaries that "define" a developing thing change—as, for instance, when sand becomes soil—then conventional reason treats sand as sand and soil as soil, much as if they were independent of each other. The *zone of interest* in this kind of rationality is a thing or phenomenon's fixity, its independence, and its basically mechanical interaction with similar or dissimilar things and phenomena. The causality that conventional reason describes, moreover, is a matter of kinetics: one billiard ball strikes another and causes them both to move from one position to another—that is to say, by means of *efficient cause*. The two billiard balls are not altered by the blow but are merely repositioned on the billiard table.

But conventional reason cannot address the problem of change at all. It views a mammal, for example, as a creature marked by a highly fixed set of traits that distinguish it from everything that is not mammalian. To "know" a mammal is to explore its structure, literally to analyze it by dismembering it, to reduce it to its components, to identify its organs and their functions, and to ascertain the way they operate together to assure the mammal's survival and reproduction. Similarly, conventional reason views a human being in terms of particular stages of the life-cycle: a person is an infant at one time, a child at another, an adolescent at still another, a youth and finally an adult. When we analyze an infant by means of conventional reason, we do not explore what it is *becoming* in the process of developing into an adult. Doubtless, when developmental psychologists and anatomists study an individual life-cycle, few of them—however conventional their rationality may be—ignore the fact that every infant is in the process of becoming an adult and that the two stages in the life-cycle are in various ways related to each other. But the principle of *A equals A* remains a basic premise. Its logical framework is the authority of consistency, and deductions almost mechanically follow from premises. Conventional reason thus serves the practical function of describing a given entity's identity and telling us how that entity is organized to be itself. But it cannot systematically explore processes of becoming, or how a living entity is patterned as a *potentiality* to phase from one stage of its development into another.

Dialectical reason, unlike conventional reason, acknowledges the developmental nature of reality by asserting in one fashion or another that *A equals not only A but also not-A*. The dialectical thinker who examines the human life-cycle sees an infant as a self-maintaining human identity while simultaneously developing into a child, from a child into an adolescent, from an adolescent into a youth, and from a youth into an adult. Dialectical reason grasps not only how an entity is organized at a particular moment but how it is organized to go beyond that level of development and become *other* than what it is, even as it retains its identity. The contradictory nature of identity—notably, that *A equals both A and not-A*—is an intrinsic feature of identity itself. The unity of opposites is, in fact, a unity qua the emerging "other," what Hegel called "the identity of identity and nonidentity."

The thinking of conventional reason today is exemplified—and disastrously reinforced—by the "true or false" questions that make up most standardized tests. One must darken a box to indicate that a statement is either "true" or "false"—and do so quickly, with minimal reflection. These tests, so commonplace today, allow for no nuanced thought or awareness of transitions. That a phenomenon or statement may well be *both true and false*—depending on its context and its place in a process of becoming other than what it is—is excluded by the logical premise on which these tests are based. This testing procedure makes for bad mental habits among young people, who are schooled to take such tests successfully, and whose careers and future lifeways depend on their scores. But the thought process demanded by such tests compartmentalizes and essentially computerizes otherwise rich minds, depriving young people of their native ability to think organically and to understand the developmental nature of the real world.

Another major presupposition of conventional reason—one that follows from its concepts of identity and causality—is that history is a layered series of separate phenomena, a mere *succession* of strata, each independent of the ones that precede and follow it. These strata may be cemented together by phases, but these phases are themselves analyzed into components and explored independently of each other. Thus, Mesozoic rock strata are independent of Cenozoic, and each stratum exists very much on its own, as do the ones that cement them together. In human history, the medieval period is independent of the modern, and the former is connected to the latter by a series of independent segments, each relatively autonomous in relation to the preceding and subsequent ones. From the standpoint of conventional reason, it is not always clear how historical change occurs or what meaning history has. Despite postmodernism and present-day historical relativism, which examine history using conventional reason and thereby ravage it, there was a time in the recent past when most historians, influenced by theories of evolution and by Marxism, regarded history as a developmental phenomenon and subsequent periods as at least depending upon prior ones. It is this tradition that dialectical reason upholds.

The intuitional approach to history is no improvement over that of conventional reason—indeed, it does the opposite: it literally dissolves historical development into an undifferentiated continuum and even into a ubiquitous, all-embracing "One." The mystical counterpart of mechanico-materialistic stratification is the reductionism that says that everything is "One" or "interconnected," that all phenomena originated from a pulse of primal energy, like the Victorian physicist who believed that when he pounded his fist on a table, Sirius trembled, however faintly. That the universe had an origin, whatever it was, does not warrant the naïve belief that the universe still "really" consists of nothing but its originating source, any more than an adult human being can be explained entirely by reference to his or her parents. This way of thinking is not far removed from the kinetic cause-effect approach of conventional reason. Nor does the "interconnectedness" of all life-forms preclude the sharp distinctions between prey and predators, or between instinctively guided life-forms and potentially rational ones. Yet these countless differentiations reflect innumerable innovations in evolutionary pathways, indeed different kinds of evolution—be they inorganic, organic, or social. Instead of apprehending things and phenomena as both differentiated and yet cumulatively related, the mystical alternative to conventional reason tends to see them, to use Hegel's famous remark, as "a night in which all cows are black."

Conventional reason, to be sure, has its useful side. Its internal consistency of propositions, irrespective of content, plays an indispensable role in mathematical thinking and mathematical sciences, in engineering, and in the nuts-and-bolts activities of everyday life. It is indispensable when building a bridge or a house; for such purposes, there is no point in thinking along evolutionary or developmental lines. If we used a logic based on anything but the principle of identity to build a bridge or a house, a catastrophe would no doubt occur. The physiological operations of our bodies, not to speak of the flight of birds and the pumplike workings of a mammalian heart, depend in great part upon the principles we associate with conventional reason. To understand or design a mechanical entity requires a form of reason that is instrumental and an analysis of reality into its components and their functioning. The truths of conventional reason, based on consistency, are useful in these areas of life. Indeed, conventional reason has contributed immeasurably to our knowledge of the universe.

For several centuries, in fact, conventional reason held out a promise to dispel the dogmatic authority of the church, the arbitrary behavior of absolute monarchs, and the frightening ghosts of superstition—and indeed, it did a great deal to fulfill this promise. But to achieve the consistency that constitutes its fundamental principle, conventional reason removes ethics from its discourse and concerns. And as an instrument for achieving certain ends, the moral character of those ends, the values, ideals, beliefs, and theories people cherish, are irrelevant to it, arbitrary matters of personal mood and taste. With its message of identity and consistency as truth, conventional reason fails us not because it is false as such but because it has staked out too broad a claim for its own validity in explaining reality. It even redefines reality to fit its claim, just as many mathematical physicists redefine reality as that which can be formulated in mathematical terms. It should come as no surprise, then, that in our highly rationalized industrial society, conventional reason has come to seem repellent. Pervasive authority, an impersonal technocracy, an unfeeling science and insensitive, monolithic bureaucracies—the very existence of all these is imputed to reason as such.

*

Here we find ourselves in something of a quandary. It is obvious that we cannot do without the much-despised tenets of conventional reason in our everyday life; nor can we do without many technologies—including sophisticated binoculars to watch birds and whales, and cameras to photograph them. This being the case, we conclude, let us turn to an irrational, mystical, or religious private world to support our moral and spiritual beliefs; let us seek communion with a mystical "One," even as we work for corporations to survive. Thus, even as we rail against dualism and plead for a greater sense of unity, we sharply dualize our own existence. Even as we may seek an elevated spirituality, communion, and connectedness, we turn to rather mundane gurus, charismatic personalities, and cultic figures who behave more like entrepreneurs in the vending of mystical nostrums than financially disinterested guides in attaining moral perfection. Even as we denounce a materialistic and consumeristic mentality, we ourselves become avid consumers of costly, supposedly spiritual or ecological products, "green" wares that bear lofty messages. Thus do the most vulgar attributes of what we regard as the realm of reason continue to invade our lives in the guise of irrational, mystical, and religious commodities.

Our mailboxes are flooded with catalogues, and our bookstores are filled with paperbacks that offer us new roads to mystical communion and a New Age into which we can withdraw and turn our backs to the harsh realities that constantly assail us. Often, this mystical withdrawal yields a state of social quietism that is more dreamlike than real, more passive than active. Preoccupied more with personal change than with social change, and concerned more with the symptoms of our powerless, alienated lives than with the root causes, we surrender control over the social aspects of our lives, even as they are so important in shaping our private lives.

But there can be no personal "redemption" without social "redemption," and there can be no ethical life without a rational life. If metaphors with mystical connotations are not to replace understanding and if obscurantism is not to replace genuine insight—all in reaction to the limitations of conventional reason and its emphasis on value-free forms of thought—we must examine the alternative form of reason that I have already introduced. This, let me insist, is not a philosophically abstract issue. It has enormous implications for how we behave as ethical beings and for our understanding of the nature of nature and our place in the natural world. Moreover, it directly affects the kind of society, sensibility, and lifeways we choose to foster.

Let us grant that the principles of identity, of efficient causality, and of stratification do apply to a particular commonsensical reality that is rendered intelligible by their use. But when we go beyond that particular reality, we can no longer reduce the rich wealth of differentiation, flux, development, organic causality, and developmental reality to a vague "One" or to an equally vague notion of "interconnectedness." A very considerable literature dating back to the ancient Greeks provides the basis of an *organic* form of reason and a *developmental* interpretation of reality.

With a few notable exceptions, the Platonic dualism of identity and change reverberated in one way or another throughout Western philosophy until the nineteenth century, when Hegel's logical works largely resolved this paradox by systematically showing that identity, or self-persistence, actually expresses itself *through* change as an ever-variegated unfolding of "unity in diversity," to use his own words.[2] The grandeur of Hegel's effort has no equal in the history of Western philosophy. Like Aristotle before him, he had an "emergent" interpretation of causality, of how the implicit becomes explicit through the unfolding of its latent form and possibilities. On a vast scale over the course of two sizable volumes, he assembled nearly all the categories by which reason explains reality, and educed one from the other in an intelligible and meaningful continuum that is graded into a richly differentiated, increasingly comprehensive, or "adequate" whole, to use some of his terms.

We may reject what Hegel called his "absolute idealism," the transition from his logic to his philosophy of nature, his teleological culmination of the subjective and objective in a god-like "Absolute," and his idea of a cosmic Spirit *(Geist)*. Hegel rarefied dialectical reason into a cosmological system that verged on the theological by trying to reconcile it with idealism, absolute knowledge, and a mystical unfolding *logos* that he often designated "God." Unfamiliar with ecology, Hegel rejected natural evolution as a viable theory in favor of a static hierarchy of Being. By the same token, Friedrich Engels intermingled dialectical reason with natural "laws" that more closely resemble the premises of nineteenth-century physics than a plastic metaphysics or an organismic outlook, producing a crude dialectical materialism. Indeed, so enamored was Engels of matter and motion as the irreducible "attributes" of Being that a kineticism based on mere motion invaded his dialectic of organic development.

To dismiss dialectical reason because of the failings of Hegel's idealism and Engels's materialism, however, would be to lose sight of the extraordinary coherence that dialectical reason can furnish and its extraordinary applicability to ecology—particularly to an ecology rooted in evolutionary development. Despite Hegel's own prejudices against organic evolution, what stands out amid the metaphysical and often theological archaisms in his work is his overall eduction of logical categories as the subjective anatomy of a developmental reality. What is needed is to free this form of reason from both the quasi-mystical and the narrowly scientistic worldviews that in the past have made it remote from the living world; to separate it from Hegel's empyrean, basically antinaturalistic dialectical idealism and the wooden, often scientistic dialectical materialism of orthodox Marxists. Shorn of both its idealism and its materialism, dialectical reason may be rendered naturalistic and ecological and conceived as a naturalistic form of thinking.

This *dialectical naturalism* offers an alternative to an ecology movement that rightly distrusts conventional reason. It can bring coherence to ecological thinking, and it can dispel arbitrary and anti-intellectual tendencies toward the sentimental, cloudy, and theistic at best and the dangerously antirational, mystical, and potentially reactionary at worst. As a way of reasoning about reality, dialectical naturalism is organic enough to give a more liberatory meaning to vague words like *interconnectedness* and *holism* without sacrificing intellectuality. It can answer the questions I posed at the beginning of this essay: what nature is, humanity's place in nature, the thrust of natural evolution, and society's relationship with the natural world. Equally important, dialectical naturalism adds an evolutionary perspective to ecological thinking—despite Hegel's rejection of natural evolution and Engels's recourse to the mechanistic evolutionary theories of a century ago. Dialectical naturalism discerns evolutionary phenomena fluidly and plastically, yet it does not divest evolution of rational interpretation. Finally, a dialectic that has been "ecologized," or given a naturalistic core, and a truly developmental understanding of reality could provide the basis for a living ecological ethics.

No general account of dialectical reason can be a substitute for reading Hegel's works on logic. For all its forced analyses and doubtful transitions in educing one logical category from another, Hegel's *Science of Logic* is dialectical reason in its most elaborate and dynamic form. This work, in many respects, absorbed the conventional logic of Aristotle's *Posterior Analytics* into the same Greek thinker's *Metaphysics*, with its bold view of the nature of reality. I shall therefore not pretend that a broad description of the dialectic can replace the detailed presentation Hegel advanced, nor try to force its theoretical unfolding into the brief "definitions and conclusions" that ordinarily pass for accounts of ideas. As Hegel himself observed in his *Phenomenology of Spirit*: "For the real issue is not exhausted by stating it as an aim, but by carrying it out; nor is the result the actual whole, but rather the result together with the process through which it came about. The aim by itself ["definitions and conclusions"] is a lifeless universal, just as the guiding tendency is a mere drive that as yet lacks an actual existence; and the bare result is the corpse which has left the guiding tendency behind it."[3] Hegel's dialectic, in effect, defies the demand for dictionary-style definition. It can be understood only in terms of the working out of dialectical reason itself, just as an insightful psychology demands that we can truly know an individual only when we know his or her entire biography, not merely the numerical results of psychological tests and physical measurements.

*

Minimally, we must assume that there is order in the world, an assumption that even ordinary science must make if it is to exist.

Minimally, too, we must assume the existence of growth and processes that lead to differentiation, not merely the kind of motion that results from push-pull, gravitational, electromagnetic, and similar forces. Finally, minimally, we must assume that there is some kind of directionality toward ever-greater differentiation or wholeness insofar as potentiality is realized in its full actuality. We need not return to medieval teleological notions of an unswerving predetermination in a hierarchy of Being to accept this directionality; rather, we need only point to the fact that there is a generally orderly development in the real world or, to use philosophical terminology, a "logical" development when a development succeeds in becoming what it is *structured* to become.

In Hegel's logical works, as in Aristotle's *Metaphysics*, dialectic is more than a remarkable "method" for dealing with reality. Conceived as the logical expression of a wide-ranging form of developmental causality, logic, in Hegel's work, joined hands with ontology. Dialectic is simultaneously a way of reasoning and an account of the objective world, with an ontological causality. As a form of reasoning, the most basic categories in dialectic— even such vague categories as "Being" and "Nothing"—are differentiated by their own inner logic into fuller, more complex categories. Each category, in turn, is a potentiality that by means of eductive thinking, directed toward an exploration of its latent and implicit possibilities, yields logical expression in the form of self-realization, or what Hegel called "actuality" *(Wirklichkeit)*.

Precisely because it is also a system of causality, dialectic is ontological, objective, and therefore naturalistic, as well as a form of reason. In ontological terms, dialectical causality is not merely motion, force, or changes of form but things and phenomena in development. Indeed, since all Being is Becoming, dialectical causality is the differentiation of potentiality into actuality, in the course of which each new actuality becomes the potentiality for further differentiation and actualization. Dialectic explicates how processes occur not only in the natural world but in the social.

How the implicit qua a relatively undifferentiated form latent with possibility becomes a more differentiated form that is true to the way its potential form is constituted is clarified in Hegel's own words. "The plant, for example, does not lose itself in mere indefinite change," he writes. It has a distinct directionality—in the case of conscious beings, purpose as will. "From the germ much is produced when at first nothing was to be seen, but the whole of what is brought forth, if not developed, is yet hidden and ideally contained within itself." It is worth noting, in this passage, that what may be "brought forth" is not necessarily developed: an acorn, for example, may become food for a squirrel or wither on a concrete sidewalk, rather than develop into what it is potentially constituted to become—notably, an oak tree. "The principle of this projection into existence is that the germ cannot remain merely implicit," Hegel goes on to observe, "but is impelled towards development, since it presents the contradiction of being only implicit."[4]

What we vaguely call the "immanent" factors that produce a self-unfolding of a development, the Hegelian dialectic regards as the contradictory nature of a being that is unfulfilled in the sense that it is only implicit or incomplete. As mere potentiality, it has not "come to itself," so to speak. A thing or phenomenon in dialectical causality remains unsettled, unstable, in tension— much as a fetus ripening toward birth strains to be born because of the way it is constituted—until it develops itself into what it "should be" in all its wholeness or fullness. It cannot remain in endless tension or "contradiction" with what it is organized to become without warping or undoing itself. It must ripen into the fullness of its being.

Modern science has tried to describe nearly all phenomena in terms of efficient cause or the kinetic impact of forces on a thing or phenomenon, reacting against medieval conceptions of causality in terms of *final cause*—notably, in terms of the existence of a deity who impels development, if only by virtue of "His" own "perfection." Hegel's notion of "imperfection"—more appropriately, of "inadequacy" or of contradiction—as an impelling factor for development partly went beyond both efficient and final notions of causality. I say "partly" for a specific reason: the philosophical archaisms that run through Hegel's dialectic weaken his position from a naturalistic viewpoint. From Plato's time until the beginning of the modern world, theological notions of perfection, infinity, and eternality permeated philosophical thought. Plato's "ideal forms" were the "perfect" and the "eternal," of which all existential things were copies. Aristotle's God, particularly as it was Christianized by the medieval Scholastics, was the "perfect" One toward which all things strove, given their finite "imperfection" and inherent limitations. In this way, a supranatural ideal defined the "imperfection" of natural phenomena and thereby dynamized them in their striving toward "perfection." There is an element of this quasi-theological thinking in Hegel's notion of contradiction: the whole course of the dialectic culminates in the "Absolute," which is "perfect" in its fullness, wholeness, and unity.

Dialectical naturalism, by contrast, conceives finiteness and contradiction as distinctly *natural* in the sense that things and phenomena are incomplete and unactualized in their development—not "imperfect" in any idealistic or supranatural sense. Until they are what they have been constituted to become, they exist in a dynamic tension. A dialectical naturalist view has nothing to do with the supposition that things or phenomena fail to approximate a Platonic ideal or a Scholastic God. Rather, they are still in the process of becoming or, more mundanely, *developing*. Dialectical naturalism thus does not terminate in a Hegelian Absolute at the end of a cosmic developmental path, but rather advances the vision of an ever-increasing wholeness, fullness, and richness of differentiation and subjectivity.

Dialectical contradiction exists within the structure of a thing or phenomenon by virtue of a formal arrangement that is incomplete, inadequate, implicit, and unfulfilled in relation to what it "should be." A naturalistic framework does not limit us to efficient causality with a mechanistic tilt. Nor need we have recourse to theistic "perfection" to explain the almost magnetic eliciting of a development. Dialectical causality is uniquely organic because it operates within a development—the degree of form of a thing or phenomenon, the way in which that form is organized, the tensions or "contradictions" to which its formal ensemble gives rise, and its metabolic self-maintenance and self-development. Perhaps the most subtle word for this kind of development is *growth*—growth not by mere accretion but by a truly immanent process of organic self-formation in a graded and increasingly differentiated direction.

A distinctive continuum emerges from dialectical causality. Here, cause and effect are not merely coexisting phenomena or "correlations," to use a common positivist term; nor are they clearly distinct from each other, such that a cause externally impacts upon a thing or phenomenon to produce an effect mechanically. Dialectical causality is cumulative: the implicit or "in itself" (an sich), to use Hegel's terminology, is not simply replaced or negated by its more developed explicit or "for itself" (für sich); rather, it is absorbed into and developed beyond the explicit into a fuller, more differentiated, and more adequate form—the Hegelian "in and for itself" (an und für sich). Insofar as the implicit is *fully* actualized by becoming what it is constituted to be, the process is truly rational, that is to say, it is fulfilled by virtue of its *internal logic*. The continuum of a development is cumulative, containing the history of its development.

*

Reality is not simply what we experience: there is a sense in which the rational has its *own* reality. Thus, there are existing realities that are irrational and unrealized realities that are rational. A society that fails to actualize its potentialities for human happiness and progress is "real" enough in the sense that it exists, but it is less than truly social. It is incomplete and distorted insofar as it merely persists, and hence it is irrational. It is less than what it should be socially, just as a generally defective animal is less than what it should be biologically. Although it is "real" in an *existential sense*, it is unfulfilled and hence "unreal" *in terms of its potentialities*.

Dialectical naturalism asks which is truly real—the incomplete, aborted, irrational "what-is," or the most fully developed, rational "what-should-be." Reason, cast in the form of dialectical causality as well as dialectical logic, yields an unconventional understanding of reality. A process that follows its immanent self-development to its logical actuality is more properly "real" than a given "what-is" that is aborted or distorted and hence, in Hegelian terms, "untrue" to its possibilities. *Reason* has the obligation to explore the potentialities that are latent in any social development and educe its authentic actualization, its fulfillment and "truth" in a new and more rational social dispensation.

It would be philosophically frivolous to embrace the "what-is" of a thing or phenomenon as constituting its "reality" without considering it in the light of the "what-should-be" that would logically emerge from its potentialities. Nor do we ordinarily do so in practice. We rightly evaluate an individual in terms of his or her known potentialities, and we form understandable judgments about whether the individual has truly "fulfilled" himself or herself. Indeed, in privacy, individuals make such self-evaluations repeatedly, which may have important effects upon their behavior, creativity, and self-esteem.

The "what-is," conceived as the strictly existential, is a slippery "reality." Accepted empirically without qualification, it excludes the past because, strictly speaking, the past no longer "is." At the same time, it yields a discontinuity with the future that— again, strictly speaking—has yet to "exist." What is more, the "what-is," conceived in strictly empirical terms, excludes subjectivity—certainly conceptual thought—from any role in the world but a spectatorial one, which may or may not be a "force" in behavior.

In the logic of a strictly empirical philosophy, mind simply registers or coordinates experience. "Reality" is a given temporal moment that exists as an experienced segment of an assumed continuum. The "real" is a frozen "here and now" to which we merely *add* an adventitious past and *presume* a future in order to experience reality intelligibly. The kind of radical empiricism advanced by David Hume replaced the notion of Being as Becoming with the experience of a given moment that renders thinking of the past as "unreal" in making inferences about the future. This kind of "reality," as Hume himself fully sensed, is impossible to live with in everyday life; hence he was obliged to define continuity, although he did so in terms of custom and habit, not in terms of causality. Conceiving immediate empirical reality as the totality of the "real" essentially banishes hindsight and foresight as little more than mere conveniences. Indeed, a strictly empirical approach dissolves the logical tissue that integrates the organic, cumulative continuity of the past with the present and that of both with the future.

By contrast, in a naturalistic dialectic, both past and future are part of a cumulative, logical, and objective continuum that includes the present. Reason is not only a means for analyzing and interpreting reality; it extends the *boundaries* of reality beyond the immediately experienced present. Past, present, and future are a cumulatively graded process that thought can truly interpret and render meaningful. We can legitimately explore such a process in terms of whether its potentialities have been realized, aborted, or warped.

In a naturalistic dialectic, the word *reality* thus acquires two distinctly different meanings. There is the immediately present empirical "reality"—or *Realität*, to use Hegel's language—that need not be the fulfillment of a potentiality, and there is the dialectical "actuality"—*Wirklichkeit*—that constitutes a complete fulfillment of a rational process. Even though *Wirklichkeit* appears as a projection of thought into a future that has yet to be existentially realized, the potentiality from which that *Wirklichkeit* develops is as existential as the world we sense in direct and immediate ordinary experience. For example, an egg patently and empirically exists, even though the bird whose potential it contains has yet to develop and reach maturity. Just so, the given potentiality of any process exists and constitutes the basis for a process that should be realized. Hence, the potentiality *does* exist objectively, even in empirical terms. *Wirklichkeit* is what dialectical naturalism *infers* from an objectively given potentiality; it is present, if only implicitly, as an existential fact, and dialectical reason can analyze and subject it to processual inferences. Even in the seemingly most subjective projections of speculative reason, *Wirklichkeit*, the "what-should-be," is anchored in a continuum that emerges from an objective potentiality, or "what-is."

Dialectical naturalism is thus integrally wedded to the objective world—a world in which Being is Becoming. Let me emphasize that dialectical naturalism not only grasps reality as an existentially unfolding continuum, but it also forms an *objective* framework for making ethical judgments. The "what-should-be" becomes an ethical criterion for judging the truth or validity of an objective "what-is." Thus ethics is not merely a matter of personal taste and values; it is factually anchored in the world itself as an objective standard of self-realization. Whether a society is "good" or "bad," moral or immoral, for example, can be *objectively* determined by whether it has fulfilled its potentialities for rationality and morality. Potentialities that are themselves actualizations of a dialectical continuum present the challenge of ethical self-fulfillment—not simply in the privacy of the mind but in the reality of the processual world. Herein lies the only meaningful basis for a truly ethical socialism or anarchism, one that is more than a body of subjective "preferences" that rest on opinion and taste.

One may well question the validity of dialectical reason by challenging the concept of *Wirklichkeit* and its claims to be more adequate than *Realität*. Indeed, I am often asked: "How do you know that what you call a distorted 'untrue' or 'inadequate' reality is not the vaunted 'actuality' that constitutes the authentic realization of a potentiality? Are you not simply making a private moral judgment about what is 'untrue' or 'inadequate' and denying the importance of immediate facts that do not support your personal notion of the 'true' and the 'adequate'?"

This question is based on the purely conventional concepts of validity used by analytical logic. "Immediate facts"— or more colloquially, "brute facts"—are no less slippery than the empirical reality to which conventional reason confines itself. In the first place, it is not relevant to determine the validity of a process by "testing" it against "brute facts" that are themselves the epistemological products of a philosophy based on fixities. A logic premised on the principle of identity, *A equals A*, can hardly be used to test the validity of a logic premised on the principle *A equals A and not-A*. The two are simply incommensurable. For analytical logic, the premises of dialectical logic are nonsense; for dialectical logic, the premises of analytical logic ossify facticity into hardened, immutable logical "atoms." In dialectical reason, "brute facts" are distortions of reality since Being is not an agglomeration of fixed entities and phenomena but is always in flux, in a state of Becoming. One of the principal purposes of dialectical reason is to explain the nature of Becoming, not simply to explore a fixed Being.

Accordingly, the validity of a concept derived from a developmental process rather than from "brute facts" must be "tested" only by examining that developmental process, particularly the structure of the potentiality from which the process emerges and the logic that can be inferred from its potentialities.

The validity of conclusions that are derived from conventional reason and experience can certainly be tested by fixed "brute facts"; hence the great success of, say, structural engineering. But to try to test the validity of actualities that derive from a dialectical exploration of potentialities and their internal logic by using "brute facts" would be like trying to analyze the emergence of a fetus in the same way that one analyzes the design and construction of a bridge. Real developmental processes must be tested by a logic of *processes*, not by a logic of "brute facts" that is analytical, based on a *datum* or fixed phenomenon.

*

I have emphasized the word *naturalism* in my account of dialectical reason not only to distinguish dialectic from its idealistic and materialistic interpretations but, more significantly, to show how it enriches our interpretation of nature and humanity's place in the natural world. To attain these ends, I feel obliged to highlight the overall coherence of dialectical reason as an abiding view of a developmental reality in its many gradations as a continuum.

If dialectical naturalism is to explain things or phenomena properly, its ontology and premises must be understood as more than mere motion and interconnection. A continuum is a more relevant premise for dialectical reason than either motion or the interdependence of phenomena. It was one of the failings of "dialectical materialism" that it premised dialectic on the nineteenth century's physics of matter and motion, from which development somehow managed to emerge. It would be just as limited to replace the entelechial processes involved in differentiation and the realization of potentiality with "interconnectedness." A dialectic based merely on a notion of "interconnected-ness" would tend to be more descriptive than eductive; it would not clearly explain how interdependencies lead to a graded entelechial development—that is, to self-formation through the self-realization of potentiality.

To assert that bison and wolves "depend" upon each other (in a seeming "union of opposites"), or that "thinking like a rock"—a vision borrowed from mystical ecology—will bring us into greater "connectedness" with the inorganic mineral world, explains little. But it explains a great deal to study how bison and wolves were differentiated in the course of evolution from a common mammalian ancestor, or how the organic world emerged from the inorganic. In the latter cases, we can learn something about how development occurs, how differentiation emerges from given potentialities, and what direction these developments follow. We also learn that a dialectical development is cumulative, namely that each level of differentiation rests on previous ones. Some developments enter directly into a given level, others are proximate to it, and still others are fairly remote. The old never completely disappears but is reworked into something new. Thus, as the fossil record tells us, mammalian hair and avian feathers are later differentiations of reptilian scales, while the jaws of all animals are a later differentiation of gills.

The nondialectical thinking that is rife in the ecology movement commonly produces such questions as "What if red-wood trees have consciousness that compares with our own?" It is fatuous to challenge dialectical reason with promiscuous "what-ifs" that have no roots in a dialectical continuum. Every intelligible "if" must itself be a potentiality that can be accounted for as the product of a development. A hypothetical "if" that floats in isolation, lacking roots in a developmental continuum, is nonsensical. As Denis Diderot's delightful character Jacques, in the picaresque dialogue *Jacques le Fataliste,* exclaimed when his master peppered him with random *if* questions: "If, if, if ... if the sea boiled, there would be a lot of cooked fish!"

The continuum that dialectical reason investigates is a highly graded, richly entelechial, logically eductive, and self-directive process of unfolding toward ever-greater differentiation, wholeness, and adequacy, insofar as each potentiality is fully actualized given a specific range of development. External factors, internal rearrangements, accidents, even gross irrationalities may distort or preclude a potential development. But insofar as order does exist in reality and is not simply imposed upon it by mind, reality has a rational dimension. More colloquially, there is a "logic" in the development of phenomena, a *general* directiveness that accounts for the fact that the inorganic did become organic, as a result of its *implicit capacity* for organicity; and for the fact that the organic did become more differentiated and metabolically self-maintaining and self-aware, as a result of potentialities that made for highly developed hormonal and nervous systems.

Stephen Jay Gould may luxuriate in the randomness—actually, the fecundity—of nature, and poststructuralists may try to dissolve both natural and social evolution into an aggregation of unrelated events, but directiveness of organic evolution unremittingly surfaces in even these rather chaotic collections of "brute facts." Like it or not, human beings, primates, mammals, vertebrates, and so forth back to the most elementary protozoans are a sequential presence in the fossil record itself, each emerging out of its preceding, if extinct, life-forms. As Gould asserts, the

Burgess Shale of British Columbia attests to a large variety of fossils that cannot be classified into a unilinear "chain of being." But far from challenging the existence of directionality in evolution toward greater subjectivity, the Burgess Shale provides extraordinary evidence of the fecundity of nature. Nature's fecundity rests on the existence of chance, indeed variety, as a *precondition* for complexity in organisms and ecosystems (as my essay "Freedom and Necessity in Nature" herein argues) and, by virtue of that fecundity, for the emergence of humanity from potentialities that involve increasing subjectivity.

Our ontological and eductive premise for dialectical naturalism, however, remains the graded continuum I have already described—and the Burgess Shale notwithstanding, human beings are not only patently *here,* but our evolution can be *explained.* Dialectical reason cuts across the grain of conventional ways of thinking about the natural world and mystical interpretations of it. Nature is not simply the landscape we see from behind a picture window, in a moment disconnected from those that preceded and will follow it; nor is it a vista from a lofty mountain peak (as I point out in my essay "Thinking Ecologically," also herein). Nature is certainly all of these things—but it is significantly more. Biological nature is above all the cumulative evolution of ever-differentiating and increasingly complex life-forms with a vibrant and interactive inorganic world. Following in a tradition that goes back at least to Cicero, we can call this relatively unconscious natural development "first nature." It is first nature in the primal sense of a fossil record that clearly leads to mammalian, primate, and human life—not to mention its extraordinary fecundity of other life-forms—and it is first nature that exhibits a high degree of orderly continuity in the actualization of potentialities that made for more complex and self-aware or subjective life-forms. Insofar as this continuity is intelligible, it has meaning and rationality in terms of its results: the elaboration of life-forms that can conceptualize, understand, and communicate with each other in increasingly symbolic terms.

In their most differentiated and fully developed forms, these self-reflexive and communicative capacities are conceptual thought and language. The human species has these capacities to an extent that is unprecedented in any other existing life-form. Humanity's awareness of itself, its ability to generalize this awareness to the level of a highly systematic understanding of its environment in the form of philosophy, science, ethics, and aesthetics, and finally, its capacity to alter itself and its environment systematically by means of knowledge and technology places it beyond the realm of the subjectivity that exists in first nature.

By singling out humanity as a unique life-form that can consciously change the entire realm of first nature, I do not claim that first nature was "made" to be "exploited" by humanity, as those ecologists critical of "anthropocentrism" sometimes charge. The idea of a *made* world has its origin in theology, notably in the belief that a supernatural being created the natural world and that evolution is infused with a theistic principle, both in the service of human needs. By the same token, humans cannot "exploit" nature, owing to a "commanding" place in a supposed "hierarchy" of nature. Words like *commanding, exploitation,* and *hierarchy* are actually *social* terms that describe how people relate to each other; applied to the natural world, they are merely anthropomorphic.

Far more relevant from the standpoint of dialectical naturalism is the fact that humanity's vast capacity to alter first nature is itself a product of natural evolution—not of a deity or the embodiment of a cosmic Spirit. From an evolutionary viewpoint, humanity has been *constituted* to intervene actively, consciously, and purposively into first nature with unparalleled effectiveness and to alter it on a planetary scale. To denigrate this capacity is to deny the thrust of natural evolution itself toward organic complexity and subjectivity—the potentiality of first nature to actualize itself in self-conscious intellectuality. One may choose to argue that this thrust was predetermined with inexorable certainty as a result of a deity, or one may contend that it was strictly fortuitous, or one may claim—as I would—that there is a natural *tendency* toward greater complexity and subjectivity in first nature, arising from the very interactivity of matter, indeed a *nisus* toward self-consciousness. But what is decisive here is the compelling fact that humanity's natural capacity to consciously intervene into and act upon first nature has given rise to a "second nature," a cultural, social, and political "nature" that today has all but absorbed first nature.

There is no part of the world that has not been profoundly affected by human activity—neither the remote fastnesses of Antarctica nor the canyons of the ocean's depths. Even wilderness areas require protection from human intervention; much that is designated as wilderness today has already been profoundly affected by human activity. Indeed, wilderness can be said to exist primarily as a result of a human decision to preserve it. Nearly all the nonhuman life-forms that exist today are, like it or not, to some degree in human custody, and whether they are preserved in their wild lifeways depends largely on human attitudes and behavior.

That second nature is the outcome of evolution in first nature and can thereby be designated as natural does not mean that second nature is necessarily creative or even fully conscious of it-self in any evolutionary sense. Second nature is synonymous with society and human internal nature, both of which are un-dergoing evolution for better or worse. Although social evolution is grounded in, indeed phases out of, organic evolution, it is also profoundly different from organic evolution. Consciousness, will, alterable institutions, and the operation of economic forces and technics may be deployed to enhance the organic world or carry it to the point of destruction. Second nature as it exists today is marked by monstrous attributes, notably hierarchy, class, the state, private property, and a competitive market economy that obliges economic rivals to grow at the expense of each other or perish. This ethical judgment, I may note, has meaning *only* if we assume that there is potentiality and self-directiveness in organic evolution toward greater subjectivity, consciousness, self-reflexivity; by inference, it is the *responsibility* of the most conscious of life-forms—humanity—to be the "voice" of a mute nature and to act to intelligent-ly foster organic evolution.

If this tendency or *nisus* in organic evolution is denied, there is no reason why the human species, like any other species, should not utilize its capacities to serve its own needs or attain its own "self-realization," to use the language of mystical ecology, at the expense of other life-forms that impede its interests and desires. To denounce humanity for "exploiting" organic nature, "degrading" it, "abusing" it, and behaving "anthropocentrically" is simply an oblique way of acknowledging that second nature is the bearer of moral responsibilities that do not exist in the realm of first nature. It is to acknowledge that if all life-forms have an "intrinsic worth" that should be respected, they have it only be-cause human intellectual, moral, and aesthetic abilities have attributed it to them—abilities that no other life-form possesses. Only human beings can even *formulate* the concept of "intrinsic worth" and endow it with ethical responsibility. The "intrinsic worth" of human beings is thus patently exceptional, indeed extraordinary.

It is essential to emphasize that second nature is, in fact, a very *unfinished,* indeed inadequate, development of nature as a whole. Hegel viewed human history as a slaughterbench. Hierarchy, class, the state, and the like are evidence—and, by no means, purely accidental evidence—of the unfulfilled potentialities of nature to actualize itself as a nature that is self-consciously creative. *Humanity as it now exists is not nature rendered self-conscious.* The future of the biosphere depends overwhelmingly on whether second nature can be *transcended* in a new system of social and organic conciliation, one that I would call "free nature"—a nature that would diminish the pain and suffering that exist in both first and second nature. Free nature, in effect, would be a conscious and ethical nature, an ecological society that I have explored in detail in my book *Toward an Ecological Society* and in the closing portions of *The Ecology of Freedom* and *Remaking Society.*

*

The last quarter of the twentieth century has witnessed an appalling regression of rationality into intuitionism, of naturalism into supernaturalism, of realism into mysticism, of humanism into parochialism, and of social theory into psychology. Metaphors replace intelligible concepts and self-interest replaces a humanistic idealism. In increasing numbers people are more concerned with finding the motives that presumably underlie expressed views than with the rational content of the views themselves. Argumentation, so necessary for the clarification of ideas, has given way to "mediation," notably the reduction of authentic intellectual differences and clashing social interests to the minimal, often trite points that all parties supposedly have in common. Accordingly, real differences are papered over with the lowest level of dialogue rather than elevated to a creative synthesis or a clear, open divergence.

To frivolously speak of "biocentrism," of "intrinsic worth," and even metaphorically, of a "biocentric democracy" (to use the deplorable verbiage of mystical ecology), as though human beings were equatable in terms of their "worth" to, say, mosquitoes—and then ask human beings to bear a moral responsibility to the world of life—is to degrade the entire project of a meaningful ecological ethics. In this book I contend that nature can indeed acquire ethical meaning—an *objectively grounded* ethical meaning. Rather than an amorphous body of personalized, often arbitrary values, this ethical meaning involves an expanded view of reality, a dialectical view of natural evolution, and a distinctive—albeit by no means hierarchical—place for humanity and society in natural evolution. The social can no longer be separated from the ecological, any more than humanity can be separated from nature. Mystical ecologists who dualize the natural and the social by contrasting "biocentrism" with "anthropocentrism" have increasingly diminished the importance of social theory in shaping ecological thinking. Political action and education have given way to values of personal redemption, ritualistic behavior, the denigration of human will, and the virtues of human irrationality. At a time when the human ego, if not personality itself, is threatened by homogenization and authoritarian manipulation, mystical ecology has advanced a message of self-effacement, passivity, and obedience to the "laws of nature," which are held to be supreme over the claims of human activity and praxis. A philosophy must be developed that breaks with this deadening aversion to reason, action, and social concern.

I have called this book *The Philosophy of Social Ecology* because I believe that a dialectical naturalism forms the underpinning of social ecology's most fundamental message: that our basic ecological problems stem from social problems. It is devoutly to be hoped that the reader will use this book as a means of entering into my works on social ecology equipped with an organic way of thinking out the problems they raise and the solutions they offer. In fact, "Thinking Ecologically" forms a direct transition from the philosophical and ethical to the social and visionary. Decades of reflection on ecological issues and ideas have taught me that philosophy, particularly a dialectical naturalism, does not inhibit our understanding of social theory and ecological problems. To the contrary, it provides us with the rational means for integrating them into a coherent whole and establishes a framework for extending this whole in more fecund and innovative directions.

—March 31, 1990

NOTES

1. The reason for my choice of the name *conventional reason* is that it encompasses two logical traditions that are often referred to interchangeably, as if they were synonyms. They are in fact distinguishable, *analytical reason* being the highly formalized and abstract logic that was elaborated out of Aristotle's *Posterior Analytics*, and *instrumental reason*, the more concrete rationality developed by the pragmatic tradition in philosophy. These two traditions meld, often unconsciously, into the commonsensical reason that most people use in everyday life; hence the word *conventional*.

2. I wish to voice a caveat here. I may be a dialectician, but I am not a Hegelian, however much I have benefited from Hegel's work. I do not believe in the existence of a cosmic Spirit *(Geist)* that finds its embodiment in the existential world or in humanity. Armed with a cosmic Spirit that elaborates itself through human history, Hegel tended to blunt the critical thrust of his dialectic and bring the "real"—the given—into conformity with the "actual"—that is, the potential. I follow out the implications of Hegel's dialectic along *naturalistic* lines. Hence my view—or my interpretation, if you like—that his project, bereft of a cosmic Spirit, provides us with a rich view of reality that includes the rational "what-should-be" as well as the often irrational "what-is." Dialectical reason is thus ontologically ethical as well as dialectically logical; a guide to rational praxis as well as a naturalistic explication of Being.

3. G.W.F. Hegel, *Phenomenology of Spirit*, trans. A. V. Miller (Oxford: Clarendon Press, 1977), pp. 2-3.

4. G.W.F. Hegel, *Lectures on the History of Philosophy*, vol. 1, trans. E. S. Haldane and Frances H. Simson (New York: Humanities Press, 1955), p. 22.

TOWARD A PHILOSOPHY
OF NATURE
The Bases for an Ecological Ethics[1]

Few philosophical areas have gained the social relevance in recent years that nature philosophy, with all its ethical implications, has acquired. A considerable segment of the literate public is now deeply occupied with seeking a philosophical interpretation of nature as a grounding for human conduct and social policy. The literature on the subject has reached truly impressive proportions and has collected a sizable public readership. In fact, it is fair to say that this interest in nature philosophy is comparable to that which Darwinian evolutionary theory generated a century ago—and it is almost equally disputatious, with equally important social implications.

But the current interest in society's relationship to nature differs basically from the continuing dispute between creationism and the theory of evolution. It emerges from a deep public concern over the ecological dislocations that uniquely mark our era. Initially, in the early and mid-seventies, this concern had a largely technocratic and legalistic focus and centered on problems of pollution, resource depletion, demography, urban sprawl, nuclear power plants, the increasing incidence of cancer—in short, the problems of conventional environmentalism.[2] Environmentalists saw these problems in strictly practical terms and considered them resolvable by legislative action, public education, and personal example.

The philosophical literature that has emerged in recent years stems from a significant popular dissatisfaction with strictly issue-oriented approaches to the current environmental crisis and reflects the need for a new theoretical turn. It addresses itself to a basically new concern: to develop an ecologically creative sensibility toward the environment, one that can serve in the highest ethical sense as a guide for human conduct and provide an awareness of humanity's "place in nature."[3] These philosophical works do not deal with nature merely as an environmental problematic; rather, they advance a vision of the natural world and raise it to the level of an inspirited metaphysical principle— without denying the significance of the environmental activism they seek to transcend. If the often narrow activism of the early and mid-seventies can be called the politics of environmentalism, the nature philosophy (which is in no way to be confused with the philosophy of science) that is surfacing so prominently today can be called its ethics, and to some degree its social conscience. Today's nature philosophies that try to bring humanity and nature into ethical commonality are meant to correct imbalances in a disequilibrated cosmos or in an irrational society.

Characteristically, the academy lags behind in this intellectualization of ecological problems. This problem is serious because the Western philosophical tradition could greatly enrich the present nature-philosophical turn; yet the academy has rendered it needlessly technical or, worse, reduced it to the production of mere historical and monographic memorabilia. Much of what passes for nature philosophy today outside the campus, therefore, tends to lack roots in the Western philosophical tradition, and such Western traditions as the ecological movement does invoke have a strongly intuitional thrust.

Nor does the academy always add clarity when it does bring its intellectual equipment to intervene in the discussion. Today, virtually all nature philosophy is burdened by a massive number of stultifying prejudices, but the worst of these prejudices fester precisely in the academy. There, any conjunction of the words nature and philosophy automatically evokes fears of antiscientific archaisms and premodernist regressions to a static cosmological metaphysics. To speak frankly, the academic mind has been trained to view nature philosophy as inimical to critical and analytical thought. No less prejudicial in this regard are the "neo-Marxists," "post-Marxists," and empirical anarchists (for whom any philosophy short of Bertrand Russell's logical atomism is sheer theology), who uneasily regard all organicist theories as redolent of either dialectical materialism or neo-fascist folk philosophies. Unless such prejudices are dispelled—or at least explored insightfully and critically—the terrain of a serious nature philosophy will be left open to mystical tendencies and intuitions that may well render any rational discussion of ecological issues impossible.

In any case, the public desire for new nature philosophies will not disappear, and the works that are appearing to satisfy this need are no less problematic than the academy's conventional wisdom on the subject. It will not do for European and American academics to disparage this trend by speckling it with learned name-droppings like "neo-Aristotelianism" or by invoking the disparate pedigrees of Schelling, Driesch, Bergson, and Heidegger.

Contemporary excursions into nature philosophy require a broader philosophical grounding than they normally receive. Unfortunately, they typically draw their nourishment more from systems theory than from the Greeks and the Germans, and their hues are tinted by Asian rather than Western cosmogonies. If such eclecticism seems discordant to academic philosophical theorists, I would argue that they must do better, rather than simply add a new set of prejudices to ones that already exist. Whether one chooses to regard recent nature-philosophical works as a loss or benefit to the ecology movement, this much is clear: if our schooled philosophical theorists turn their backs on the rising theoretical interest in the meaning of nature and humanity's place in it, they will merely cut themselves off further from some of the most important developments in contemporary society.

Before we turn to the widely disparate theorists of popular nature philosophies, we must deal with a problem that unceasingly nags the academic acolytes of modern scientism. Like a troubling and eruptive unconscious, it plagues the philosophical superego of the academy and some of its self-professed radical theorists. This philosophical unconscious is "the Tradition," or what is more arrogantly called the "archaic" background that predates Enlightenment—indeed, modern—philosophy. Modern subjectivistic and scientistic orientations have raised a barrier against pre-Enlightenment philosophy that permits little of it to filter through, so that its own origins have become a mystery to Western philosophy, a frightening specter like the primal nightmares of childhood that haunt the armored ego of the adult. True, interest in Aristotle's *Metaphysics* "remains perennial," as we are told, and "does not flag or fail with the passing years, no matter how far the fashion of thought current at the moment may seem to wander from the confines of Aristotelian tradition."[4] But apart from such canonical works, the censor that acts like a screen on earlier philosophies seems remarkably secure. Heidegger capitalized on this failure (regrettably, in my view) and delved into the originating thinkers of Western philosophy, arguing that they are worthy of serious exegesis (although not all of Heidegger's "woodpaths" are to be followed).[5] Ontology understandably bears a fearsome visage when it lacks a social and moral context, and the concept of Being loses contact with reality when it is subtly assimilated to subjective approaches to reality like Heidegger's.

Limitations of space make it impossible for me to fully explore the problems that my remarks on these prejudices doubtless raise. But even some of the best-known theorists of nature philosophy in the ecology movement today commit an error. Although they may be cognizant of the prejudices and the censoring mechanisms that separate contemporary philosophy from its own history, they have dug their trenches poorly by defining themselves against Descartes rather than Kant.

This is by no means an academic issue, nor is it strictly a philosophical one. The emphasis on Cartesian mechanism as the original sin that distorted the modern image of nature has been overstated for reasons that are more programmatic than theoretical. Villainous as Descartes may seem, it is a certain realpolitik, I suspect, that demonizes him over Kant. For to single out Kant would necessitate challenging the dubious subjectivism—such as the subjectivism that Gregory Bateson gives to systems theory— and quasi-religious transcendentalism now burgeoning in so much contemporary "antimechanistic" thinking. As a result, philosophical theories of nature and the objective ecological ethics derived from them are being created in the false light of the "epistemological turn" that Kant ultimately gave to Western philosophy. The ontologically oriented pre-Kantian interpretations of nature remain as ambiguous in the ecology movement as in the academy.

But premodern and particularly Presocratic philosophy is not the dead dog that conventional philosophy depicts it as being. I am not concerned, for the present, with the *specific* speculations that pre-Kantian philosophies advanced—particularly those of the Presocratics. Rather, I am concerned with their *intentions* and with the *kind* of unities they tried to foster. What is important, as Gregory Vlastos has so admirably emphasized, is that they authentically voiced an objectivity permeated by ethics. Indeed, in contrast to the naturalism that became so fashionable in American academies during the 1930s and 1940s, the unifying feature of the Ionian, Eleatic, Heraclitean, and Pythagorean trends is precisely their conviction that the universe had in some sense a moral character irrespective of human purposes. So alien is this proposition to the post-Kantian era that it is dismissed as "archaic" and "teleological" almost as a knee-jerk reaction.[6] Yet one cannot simply dismiss the fact that such great themes as Being, Form, Motion, and Causality were once infused with moral meaning. In fact, they permeate speculative philosophy to this day. The *various* ways in which the Presocratics explained the *arche* of the world followed out the logic of this moral meaning.

The very ability to know implies that the world is orderly and intelligible and that it lends itself to rational interpretation because it is rational. From Thales to Hegel, philosophy consistently retained this essential orientation. As Lawrence J. Henderson wrote in his immensely influential 1912 work *The Fitness of the Environment*, the "idea of purpose and order are among the first concepts regarding their environment which appear, a vague anticipation of philosophy and science, in the minds of men." For Henderson, to be sure, it was the "advent of modern science" that validated universal order—in the form of natural law; Darwin's hypothesis of natural selection, in turn, validated natural law "as the basis of purpose," specifically the "new scientific concept of fitness," and thereby rescued speculative thought from the "dogma of final causes."[7] But what is important in Henderson's remarks is that he regards the world as intelligible, not the specific content of that intelligibility.

Hellenic thought, by the same token, was pointedly moral *insofar as it saw the world as rational*—that is, its rationality and intelligibility were *equivalent* to its morality. However intuitively or consciously, the Hellenic notion of *nous*—mind—constituted the world or inhered in it. Precisely because one could explain the world, the world was meaningful. Nor did Presocratic thought stop at partial explanations of order; it tried to explain it to the fullest. Accounts of the *arche* of the world—its active substance— are redolent with meaning, such as water (which perhaps alludes to kinship) and the "unbounded" or *"aer"* (which historians of Greek philosophy now regard as "soul," the "breath of life").

This sense of reality as pregnant, fecund, and immanently self-elaborating still provides direction for an ecological philosophy, however arguable the nature philosophies of the pre-Kantian past may be. Of particular interest here are the Presocratics. Emphasis on the Presocratics' "naïveté," their "ontological need" (to use one of Theodor Adorno's many unfortunate phrases), and their "monism" has all too cheaply obscured this possibility. That Presocratic thought was riddled by demonstrably false archaisms is beside the point. It is its orientation that concerns us, not its ontological merits, and its animistic aspects are such as might be expected in a transition from the mythopoeic world to the world of Plato and Aristotle. And in contrast to Heidegger, we should not view the Presocratics as having an "authentic," prelapsarian relationship with Being but as points of departure for the richer philosophical insights of Plato, Aristotle, and the other philosophers who constitute the Western philosophical tradition. *My high valuation of the Presocratics here is purely heuristic:* I do not intend to argue for their notion of "cosmic justice"— which was patently an extrapolation of the democratic *polis* into the natural world—or for adherence to their view that nature is "just" in any other sense. Rather, I wish to emphasize the importance of searching for values that can be grounded in nature— more basically, in natural evolution.

Despite their "naïveté," the Pythagorean *arche*—form—and ideals of limit, *kosmos* (order combined with beauty), and *krasis* (equilibrium) have a remarkable, indeed alluring richness. The Pythagorean notion of form, for example, is essential for understanding holism, for it adds the formal concept of *arrangement* to the numerical notion of *sum*. The notion of form as the expression of the good and the beautiful renders virtue cosmically immanent.

More radically, the Presocratics anchored their interpretation of nature in the notion of *isonomia* (equality), which includes the equality of the very elements that make up the world. Philosophers from Anaximander to Empedocles had a thoroughgoing respect for a ubiquitous principle of equality. So consciously did they hold the principle, that Alcmaeon used the term *monarchy* with opprobrium to characterize the "mastery" or "supremacy" of one cosmic power over another. *Krasis* is not the mechanical equipoise of contrasting powers but, more organically, their blending and, in the sequence of phenomena (initially, in Greek medical theory), their rotation. "As in the democratic *polis* 'the demos rules by turn,' so the hot could prevail in summer without injustice to the cold, if the latter had its turn in the winter," Vlastos observes, highlighting the parallels between the Athenian political system and this notion. "And if a similar and concurrent cycle of successive supremacy could be assumed to hold among the powers in the human body, then the *krasis* of man and nature would be perfect."[8]

Empedocles thoroughly naturalized this "elegant tissue of assumptions," as Vlastos calls these parallels between society and nature. His concept of "roots" as distinguished from "elements," undifferentiated "Being," and "atoms" vastly enlarged the implicit Hellenic notion of an immanently generative nature to a point unsurpassed even by Aristotle. The "roots," as Francis Cornford observes, are "equal in status or lot"; they rotate their "rule" with their own unique "honor," for in no case is the universe a "monarchy" and none of its powers can claim even the primacy that Thales gave to fluidity and Anaximenes to soul.[9]

Presocratic thought was consciously infused by a far-reaching notion of cosmic justice, or *dikaisyne*. This concept of justice extends beyond social and personal issues to nature itself. For the Presocratics, "justice is no longer inscrutable moira, imposed by arbitrary forces with incalculable effect. Nor is she the goddess Dike, moral and rational enough, but frail and unreliable." Unlike Hesiod's Dike, this justice is one with nature itself and "could no more leave the earth than the earth could leave its place in the firmament."[10] Its opposite, *adikaisyne,* marks every transgression of cosmic justice—of the law of the measure and the *peras* or limit of things and relationships. It demands reparation and the restoration of harmony.

Nature, in effect, appeared as a commonwealth, a *polis,* whose *isonomia* effaced the "distinctions between two grades of being—divine and mortal, lordly and subservient, noble and mean, of higher and lower honor. It was the ending of these distinctions that made nature autonomous and therefore completely and unexceptionally 'just.' Given a society of equals, it was assumed, justice was sure to follow, for none would have the power to dominate the rest. This assumption ... had a strictly physical sense. It was accepted not as a political dogma but as a theorem in physical inquiry. It is, none the less, remarkable evidence of the confidence which the great age of Greek democracy possessed in the validity of the democratic idea—a confidence so robust that it survived translation into the first principles of cosmology and medical theory."[11]

*

Naïve as the Presocratic view may be with all its archaisms, a nature philosophy that is more than the simple contest between mechanism and organicism encountered today would serve to clarify the wayward fortunes of Western philosophy and challenge the limits it has imposed on ecological ethics. Ironically, the founders of modern science—Copernicus, Kepler, and Tycho Brahe—were raging Pythagoreans. What early Renaissance thought and science rescued from the ancients was not *isonomia* but form, as well as the shared premise of all speculative reason that nature is an intelligible *kosmos*. Descartes never challenged this conceptual framework—he merely gave it a mechanical form, alluring and subversive for its time.

It was Kant—a near Jacobin—who made the most significant turn in Western philosophy with his "Copernican revolution," the "epistemological turn." Kant finally denatured nature of its Presocratic remnant by removing the material "grade of being" altogether. Things-in-themselves ceased to be things at all for cognitive purposes, and one grade of Being effectively ceased to exist. Kant left us alone with our own subjectivity. "Kant does not, like all earlier philosophers, investigate objects," as Karl Jaspers incisively summarized the issue; "what he inquires into is our knowledge of objects. He provides no doctrine of the metaphysical world, but a critique of the reason that aspires to know it. He gives no doctrine of Being as something objectively known, but an elucidation of existence as the situation of our consciousness. Or, in his own words, he provides no 'doctrine,' but a 'propaedeutics.'" Accordingly, Kantian categories have objective validity only insofar as they remain within the limits of possible experience. After Kant, "metaphysics in the sense of objective knowledge of the supersensible or as ontology, which teaches being as whole, is impossible."[12]

As liberating as this innovation was from absolute empiricism, which renders its own experience in a world of pure

Being, it was not liberating from absolutes generally. Kant himself made a sweeping intellectualization of objectivity. Although he acknowledged a noumenal world that is "supersensible" or "unknowable" and that constitutes the originating source of the perceptions that his categories synthesize into authentic knowledge, he opened the way to an epistemological focus on *systems of knowledge* rather than a naturalistic focus on *systems of facts*. Facticity itself was absorbed within systems of knowledge, and the Greek *onta*, the "really existing things," were displaced by *episteme*, our "knowledge" of the now "unknowable" *onta*. Hegel ridiculed the patent contradiction of knowing that an "unknowable" was unknowable—but Kant had dug a veritable trench around philosophy that excluded nature as ontology and that rendered thought into Being. With Kant's agnostic and essentially skeptical outlook, his epistemological turn became absolutized in philosophy.

Lost in this development were the *onta* that alone constitute the underpinnings of nature philosophy, which now had to be distinguished from Kantian philosophies of the nature of knowing.[13] Hegel heaped scorn on the notion of the thing-in-itself, whose very thinghood by definition requires determinations and in fact bears the imprint of the Kantian categories. But even Hegel ended in the subjectivity of the Absolute. For Hegel, after all the toil of Spirit, object and subject finally come to rest in Mind—in knowledge as self-knowing in all its totality—and it was not for sentimental reasons that Hegel's *Encyclopedia* ended with a quotation from Aristotle that exults "thought [that] thinks on itself because it shares the notion of the object of thought."[14] A century later, Husserl's process of *epoché* bracketed out the natural world in order to establish the logical necessity on which it ultimately hangs; Heidegger regarded *Dasein* as the human existent and royal road to Being. Both distilled reality into intellection, and the formalizations of the human mind became the exclusive point of entry into Being. Only insofar as these formalizations become Being itself can one call Heidegger's or Husserl's philosophical strategy ontological.

Nor has ecological philosophy breached the Kantian trench. Rather, it is a captive within it without even knowing it. Gregory Bateson, the most widely read of its gurus, makes an almost wholly subjective interpretation of the notorious Mind-Nature relationship. In trying to "build the bridge" between "form and substance," Bateson emphasizes only too correctly that Western science began with the "wrong half" of the chasm—atomistic materialism. Today many ecologically oriented readers are attracted to his supplantation of matter with mind and to his conjoining of fact (whatever that means for him) with value. But quite systematically, Bateson turns any interrelational system at all into "Mind" and hence makes it subjective. (This notion also feeds into quasi-supernaturalistic visions of reality—generally Eastern in origin—which curiously tend to transcend the natural world rather than explain it.) That "Mind is empty; it is no-thing," for Bateson, means literally that it is no *thing* at all. Hence, only "ideas are immanent, embodied in their examples. And the examples [the material embodiments of ideas] are, again, no-things. The claw, as an example, is not the *Ding an sich;* it is precisely not the *'thing in itself.'* Rather, it is what mind makes of it, namely, an *example* of something or other."[15]

This is not merely a subjectivist variant of Kantianism; it is a denial of thinghood as such. A true son of the epistemological turn, Bateson claims that "all experience is subjective ... our

brains make the images that we think we 'perceive.'" Indeed, "oc-
cidental culture" lives under the "illusion" that its own "visual
image of the external world" has ontological reality. Even as
Bateson dismisses ontological properties as such, he smuggles
them back into his own work as systems. Although his argument
against "atomies" takes on the appearance of an argument
against presuppositions, Bateson's own view is actually over-
loaded with presuppositions—his whole thesis, he says elsewhere, is "based on the premise that mental function is immanent
in the interaction of differentiated 'parts.'"[16]

Batesonian mentalism is nourished by the cybernetic idea
that perceptions are parts of a system, not isolates, or as Bateson
calls them, "atomies." He intends this to mean that the differentiae that form an aggregate of interacting parts are not spatial,
temporal, or substantial; they are relational. The interaction between a subject and object forms a kind of unit system that exists
within ever-larger systems, be they communities, societies, the
planet, the solar system, or ultimately the universe. Bateson
designates these systems as "Minds"—or more precisely, as a
hierarchy of "Minds," much like Arthur Koestler's "holarchy,"
with its sublevels of "holons" that extend from subatomic par-
ticles, through atoms, molecules, organelles, cells, tissues, and organs, up to living organisms, which have their own scala
naturae.[17]

Bateson's view that context fixes meaning is not very new
if one knows anything about Whitehead. But cybernetics, too, is
uncritically presupposed. That cybernetics could simply be
another form of mechanism—electronic rather than mechanical—eludes him, as it seems to elude most of its acolytes. Feedback loops are as mechanistic as flywheels, however different the

physics involved may be. Cyberneticians engage in a reductionism similar to that which guided mechanical thinking in Newton's day, except that Newton's was based on matter rather than energy. The ecological cybernetics of Howard Odum, whose tunnel vision perceives only the flow of calories through an ecosystem, is as shallow philosophically as it is useful practically within its own narrow limits. For its more mystical acolytes, cybernetics combines with Eastern and Native American spirituality to become a "spiritual mechanism" that eerily parallels the failings of materialist mechanism, without the latter's contact with reality. A deadening vocabulary of *information, inputs, outputs, feedback,* and *energy*—terminology largely born from wartime research on radar and servo-mechanisms for military guidance systems[18]—replaces such once-vibrant words as *knowledge, dialogue, explanation, wisdom,* and *vitality.*

As critics of Bateson's view and of cybernetics generally have been quick to point out, hierarchies of "Mind" have authoritarian implications.[19] Koestler was acutely conscious of this problem in his notion of "holarchy," with its hierarchies of "holons";[20] but Bateson, if anything, is given to using examples that accentuate the authoritarian features of his outlook. As Bateson describes "an alternating ladder of calibration and feedback up to larger and larger spheres of relevance and more and more abstract information and wider decision," he warns that

> within the system of police and law enforcement, and indeed in all hierarchies, it is most undesirable to have direct contact between levels that are nonconsecutive. It is not good for the total organization to have a pipeline of communication between the

driver of the automobile [who is ticketed for violating a speed limit] and the state police chief. Such communication is bad for the morale of the police force. Nor is it desirable for the policeman to have direct access to the legislature, which would undermine the authority of the police chief. ... In legal and administrative systems, such jumping of logical levels is called *ex post facto* legislation. In families, the analogous errors are called *double binds*. In genetics, the Weissmannian barrier which prevents the inheritance of acquired characteristics seems to prevent disasters of this nature. To permit direct influence from somatic state to genetic structure might destroy the hierarchy of organization within the creature.[21]

This is sociobiology with a vengeance. Nor was one of the outstanding founders of systems theory, Ludwig von Bertalanffy, immune to this tendency when he observed that "the behavior of animals such as rats, cats, and monkeys provides the necessary bases for interpretation and control of human behavior; what appears to be special in man is secondary and ultimately to be reduced to biological drives and primary needs."[22]

Bertalanffy's "general system theory"—with which he seeks to replace Cartesian mechanism, "one-way causality," and "unorganized complexity"—hardly solves the problems that cybernetic mechanism raises. Ultimately, the thinking in both cases is similar: a general system theory based on a worldview of "organized complexity" is essentially a cybernetic system that is "open" rather than "closed." Bertalanffy admits that general system theory "is still mechanistic in the sense that it presupposes a 'mechanism,' that is, structural arrangements." Although it is quite true that "in behavioral parlance, the cybernetic model is the familiar S-R [stimulus-response] ... scheme" and simply replaces *"linear causality"* with *"circular causality* by way of the feedback loop," the claims advanced by a general system theory to encompass "multivariable interaction, maintenance of wholes in the counteraction of component parts, multilevel organization into systems of ever higher order, differentiation, centralization, progressive mechanization, steering and trigger causality, regulation, evolution toward higher organization, teleology and goal-directedness in various forms and ways, etc.," are generally more programmatic than real and incorporate some of the most authoritarian and mechanistic attributes of cybernetics. That the "elaboration of this program has only just begun ... and is beset with difficulties" is an understatement.[23]

The issue of development—specifically evolution—is crucial to nature philosophy, but a solution to the problem of why development occurs, why order and complexity emerge from lesser degrees of order and simplicity, remains markedly absent from systems theory. None of the systems theories come close to an explanation of development, and it is not at all clear that the explanatory powers of cybernetics and systems theory can encompass it. To my knowledge, the only "breakthrough" in this regard that lends credibility to Bertalanffy's sweeping claims for the explanatory potential of general system theory has been Ilya Prigogine's mathematical elaboration of the organizing role of positive feedback.[24] Prigogine's work essentially utilizes the symmetry-breaking effects of positive feedback (or more bluntly, disorder) as a means for creating "order" at various levels of organization.

As valuable as this approach may be within the realm of systems theory itself, particularly in its applications to chemistry, the spontaneous structuration that it describes does so as the result of causes no less mechanistic than Bateson's ladder of "Minds" and Koestler's hierarchy of "holons." Certainly, no systems theory I have cited explains *why* one "level of organization" supersedes or incorporates another; at best, they describe only *how*, and even these descriptions are woefully incomplete. Bateson's stochastic strategy for "explaining" sequence, for example, merely correlates random genetic mutations (or worse, point mutations, which are piecemeal as well as random) with a "selective process" that is remarkably passive. Natural selection merely tells us that the "fittest" survive environmental changes. If all we know about evolutionary development is that amidst a flurry of utterly random mutations, the organisms that are capable of surviving are those that are the "fittest" to survive—a circular thesis—then we know very little about evolution indeed.

It is not clear whether cybernetics and systems theory can extend beyond mere *interaction,* as distinguished from authentic *development.* We certainly have no "system" or "Mind" other than mere interaction that explains it in these theories. An "interaction" cannot be construed as a relationship unless it is meaningful. To call the mere physical fact that one human being stumbles over another "intersubjectivity," for example, degrades the very meaning of the word *subjective.* The encounter of one body with another merely produces a form of physical contact. The "interaction" becomes "intersubjective" only when the two persons address each other—possibly with friendly recognition, possibly with expletives, possibly even with blows. Moreover, in view of recent "formalizations" of even radical social theories, I cannot emphasize too strongly that attempting to understand this "interaction" in all its possible forms and meanings requires knowing the social and psychological context in which it occurred—that is to say, the history or dialectic, however trivial, that lies buried within the "intersubjectivity" that results from the "interaction."

*

We can certainly criticize cybernetics' misuse of the concept of *hierarchy*—a strictly social term—to refer to degrees of complexity and organization. But ultimately, cybernetics and systems approaches to ecological issues are not subject to immanent critique. Like Kantian and neo-Kantian philosophies, they are basically self-sufficient and self-enclosed. Although Kant's conclusions do not follow completely from his premises, his very errors have served as correctives for his successors. Translated into the language of systems theory, Kantianism and its subjective sequelae are sufficiently closed that their errors become the self-corrective source of perpetuating Kant's "Copernican revolution."

That Kant's epistemological turn greatly broadened philosophical thought is hardly arguable. Kant's elaboration of an epistemology and the introduction of the subject as both observer and participant in cohering knowledge and reality filled a major lacuna in Western philosophy. Definitely arguable, however, are the imperial claims that this subjectivism advanced, the totalization of reality and the arrogant exclusivity it staked out for itself. Hegel's brilliant criticism of Kant, while indubitably shrewd, did not damage these imperial claims; indeed, to some degree it performed a corrective function for neo-Kantians of later generations.

If subjectivistic approaches to nature and those based on systems theory must be challenged, we are obliged to formulate new premises that provide coherence and meaning to natural evolution. The truth or falsity of a nature philosophy will lie in the truth or falsity of its description of an unfolding reality—in *evolution*, as we are beginning to know it in nature today, and as this natural evolution grades into social evolution and ethics. We must not, however, once again rear the hoary myth of a "presuppositionless philosophy" but choose our presuppositions carefully and adequately so that they impart coherence and meaning.

Our first presupposition is that we have the right to *attribute* properties to nature based on the best of our knowledge, the right to assume that certain attributes as well as contexts are *self-evident* in nature. This assumption is immediately problematic for a vast number of academic philosophers—although, ironically, it is no problem for most scientists. The great Renaissance notion that "matter" and "motion" are basic attributes of nature, its most underlying properties (just as metabolism is a basic property of life), remains a prevalent *scientific* assumption well into our own time, however much the meanings of the terms *matter* and *motion* have changed.

It remained for Diderot in his extraordinary *D'Alembert's Dream* to propose the crucial trait of nature that transforms mere motion into development and directiveness: the notion of *sensibilité*, an internal *nisus*, that is commonly translated as "sensitivity."[25] This immanent fecundity of "matter"—as distinguished from motion as mere change of place—scored a marked advance

over the prevalent mechanism of La Mettrie and, by common ac-
knowledgement, anticipated nineteenth-century theories of
evolution and, in my view, recent developments in biology. Yet
D'Alembert's Dream's very title forewarns readers of Diderot's can-
did sense of doubt of his own "likely story," given the limited
scientific knowledge of the time.

Sensibilité implies an active concept of matter that yields
increasing complexity, from the atomic level to the brain. Continuity is preserved through this development without any
reductionism; indeed, in the scala naturae dynamized by
Diderot's avowed Heraclitean bias for flux, there is a *nisus* for
complexity, an *entelechia* that emerges from the very nature,
structure, and form of potentiality *itself*, given varying degrees
of the organization of "matter." From this potentiality and the
actualization of the potentialities of various organisms, *sensibilité*
initiates its journey of self-actualization and emergent form.
Diderot's holism, in turn, is one of the most conspicuous features of *D'Alembert's Dream*. An organism achieves its unity and
sense of direction from the contextual wholeness of which it is
part, a wholeness that imparts directiveness to the organism and
reciprocally receives directiveness from it.

Apart from their systematic and mathematical treatment of
feedback, cybernetics and systems theory can add little to this
idea, advanced by an authentic and largely unacknowledged
genius who died almost two centuries ago. Not only did the active and directive "matter" that Diderot advanced with his notion
of *sensibilité* mark a radical breach with Renaissance and Enlightenment mechanism, but its relevance as "sensitivity," however metaphoric the terminology, is radically important for
understanding current developments in natural science.

A second presupposition is the *alternative* pathway to Kantianism that Hegel opened up with his own phenomenological strategy in the richly dialectical approach of the *Phenomenology of Spirit*. In Hegel's own description of this strategy: insofar as the *Phenomenology* "has only phenomenal knowledge for its object, this exposition seems not to be Science, free and self-moving in its own peculiar shape; yet from this standpoint it can be regarded as the path of the natural consciousness which presses forward to true knowledge; or as the way of the Soul which journeys through the series of its own configurations as though they were the stations appointed for it by its own nature, so that it may purify itself for the life of the Spirit, and achieve finally, through a completed experience of itself, the awareness of what it really is in itself." This "pressing forward" is immanent to true knowledge, for short of finding its goal, "no satisfaction is to be found at any of the stations along the way."[26]

Like Lukács, and unlike the academic fluff who have vitiated Hegel's strong reality principle, I share Engels's view that the *Phenomenology* may be regarded as "a parallel of the embryology and the paleontology of the mind, a development of individual consciousness through its different stages, set in the form of an abbreviated reproduction of the stages through which the consciousness of man has passed in the course of history."[27] To a remarkable extent, although by no means consistently, the self-movement of consciousness in the *Phenomenology* parallels the self-movement of consciousness in historical reality, although the strategy is captive to rational reality and the ethical universe it opens for ecology.

Taking as our presuppositions Diderot's concept of *sensibilité* in "matter" and Hegel's phenomenological strategy, we emerge with a fascinating possibility. Speaking metaphorically, it is nature itself that seems to "write" natural philosophy and ethics, not logicians, positivists, neo-Kantians, and heirs of Galilean scientism. According to a fairly recent revolution in astrophysics (possibly comparable to the achievements of Copernicus and Kepler), the cosmos is opening itself up to us in new ways that demand an exhilaratingly speculative turn of mind and a more qualitative approach to natural phenomena than in the past. It is becoming increasingly tenable to hold that the entire universe is the cradle of life—not merely our own planet or possibly planets like it. The formation of all the elements from hydrogen and helium, their combination into small molecules and later into self-forming macromolecules, and finally the organization of these macromolecules into the constituents of life and possibly mind follow a sequence that challenges Bertrand Russell's image of humanity as an accidental spark in a meaningless void. The presence of complex organic molecules in the vast reaches of the universe is replacing the classical image of space as a void with an understanding of space as a restlessly active chemogenic ground for an astonishing sequence of increasingly complex chemical compounds. Recent theories about the formation of DNA that are modeled on the activity of crystalline replication (a notion advanced as early as 1944 by Erwin Schrödinger) suggest how genetic guidance and evolution itself might have emerged to form an interface between the inorganic and organic.[28]

The point is that we can no longer be satisfied with the theory of an inert "matter" that fortuitously aggregates into life. The universe bears witness to a *developing*—not merely moving—substance, whose most dynamic and creative attribute is its unceasing capacity for self-organization into increasingly complex forms. Form plays a central role in this developmental and growth process, while function is an indispensable correlate. The orderly universe that makes science possible and its highly concise logic—mathematics—meaningful presupposes the correlation of form with function.

In life—a *graded* development beyond the chemogenic crucible that we call the universe—metabolism and development establish another elaboration of *sensibilité:* symbiosis. Recent data support the applicability of Peter Kropotkin's mutualistic naturalism not only to relationships between species but among complex cellular forms. As biologist William Trager ironically remarked a decade ago about the "struggle for existence" and the "survival of the fittest": "few people realize that mutual cooperation between different kinds of organisms—symbiosis—is just as important, and that the 'fittest' may be the one that most helps another to survive."[29]

Indeed, the cellular structure of all multicellular organisms is itself testimony to a symbiotic arrangement that renders complex life-forms possible. The eukaryotic cell—a cell that makes up an organism—is a highly functional symbiotic arrangement of the less complex and more primal prokaryotes, or single-celled organisms, and evolved in an anaerobic world long before our highly oxygenated atmosphere was formed. The work of Lynn Margulis gives us reason to believe that eukaryotic flagella derived from anaerobic spirochetes; that mitochondria derived from prokaryotic bacteria that were capable of respiration as well as fermentation; and that plant chloroplasts derived from blue-green algae (cyanobacteria).[30]

If Manfred Eigen is correct that evolution "appears to be an inevitable event, given the presence of certain matter with specified autocatalytic properties and under the maintenance of the finite (free) energy flow [solar energy] necessary to compensate for the steady production of energy," then our very concept of matter has to be radically revised.[31] The prospect that life and all its attributes are latent in matter as such, that biological evolution is deeply rooted in symbiosis or mutualism, suggests that what we call matter is actually active substance.

The traditional dualism between the living and nonliving worlds, between organisms and their abiotic ecosystems, is being replaced with the more challenging notion that life "makes much of its own environment," to use Margulis's words. From an ecological viewpoint, in which life is in its environment and not isolated from it, the Weissmannian barrier that conveniently separates genetic from somatic changes ceases to be meaningful. "Certain properties of the atmosphere, sediments, and hydrosphere are controlled by and for the biosphere"; by comparing lifeless planets such as Mars and Venus with the Earth, Margulis notes that the high concentration of oxygen in our atmosphere is anomalous in contrast with the carbon dioxide atmospheres of other planets. Moreover, "the concentration of oxygen in the Earth's atmosphere remains constant in the presence of nitrogen, methane, hydrogen, and other potential reactants." Life-forms, in effect, play an active role in maintaining a relatively constant supply of free oxygen molecules in the Earth's atmosphere. If the anomalies of the Earth's atmosphere "are far from random," much the same can be said for the temperature of the Earth's surface and the salinity of its oceans, whose stability seems to be a function of life on the planet. The "natural selection" of Darwinian evolution may itself be the product of life-forms, which presumably filter out some genetic changes.[32]

Even the Modern Synthesis, the neo-Darwinian model of organic evolution that has been in force since the early 1940s, has been challenged as too narrow and perhaps too mechanistic in its outlook. Its thesis of slow-paced evolutionary change emerging from the interplay of small variations, which are "selected" for their adaptability to the environment, is no longer as tenable as it once seemed based on the fossil record. Evolution seems instead to have been rather more sporadic, marked by occasional changes of considerable rapidity, then long periods of stasis. The "Effect Hypothesis," advanced by Elizabeth Vrba, suggests that evolution includes an immanent striving, not merely random mutational changes filtered by external selective factors. As one observer notes, "Whereas species selection puts the forces of change on environmental conditions, the Effect Hypothesis looks to internal parameters that affect the rates of speciation and extinction."[33]

Indeed, the theory of small, gradual point mutations (a theory that accords with the Victorian notion of strictly fortuitous evolutionary change, much like the Victorian image of the economic marketplace) can be challenged on genetic grounds alone. Not only genes but chromosomes, too, may be altered chemically and mechanically. Genetic changes may range from "simple" point mutations, through jumping genes and transposable elements, to major chromosomal rearrangements. Major morphological changes may thus result from mosaics of genetic change. This dynamic raises the intriguing possibility of a directiveness to genetic change itself, not simply a promiscuous and purely fortuitous randomness, and an environment largely created by life itself, not by forces exclusively external to it.

Neither mysticism nor anthropocentrism is involved in an ecological view that ontologically grades natural history into social history without sacrificing the unity of either. Nor is it a supernatural fallacy to ultimately derive the human brain from an actively chemogenic universe that is self-forming and immanently entelechial. Although Hans Driesch gave entelechy a bad name, the concept derives from Aristotle, not from Driesch's confused neovitalism.

The fallacies of classical Greek cosmology generally lie less in its ethical orientation than in its dualistic view of nature. For all its emphasis on speculation at the expense of experimentation, ancient cosmology erred most when it tried to join the self-organizing, fecund nature it had inherited from the Ionians with a vitalizing force alien to the natural world itself. The self-organizing properties of nature were replaced with Parmenides' Dike—like Bergson's *élan vital*, a latently dualistic cosmology that could not trust nature to develop on its own spontaneous grounds, any more than ruling social and political strata trust the body politic to manage its own affairs.

These archaisms, with their theological nuances and their tightly formulated teleologies, have been justly viewed as socially reactionary traps. They tainted the works of Aristotle and Hegel as surely as they mesmerized the medieval Schoolmen. Classical nature philosophy erred not in its project of trying to elicit an ethics from nature, but in the spirit of domination that poisoned it from the start with an often authoritarian, supernatural arbiter who weighed and corrected the imbalances or "injustices" that erupted in nature. The ancient gods were still worshipped in the classical era, even after Heraclitus; they had to be exorcised by the Enlightenment before an ethical continuum between nature and humanity could be rendered more meaningful and "democratic." Late Renaissance thought initiated a new, more rational connection between nature and humanity. Beginning with Galileo and the new scientific societies that were emerging, the way was opened to the increasingly democratic participation of everyone in the discovery of truth. All men—and later women—could now participate in unearthing knowledge, and the veracity of the facts they discovered could be judged freely by the merits of their work, not by their social status.

Today, we may well be able to permit nature—not Dike, God, Spirit, or an *élan vital*—to open itself up to us as the ground for an ethics on its own terms. Contemporary science's greatest achievement is the growing evidence it provides that randomness is subject to a directive ordering principle. Mutualism is a good by virtue of its function in fostering the evolution of natural variety and complexity. We require no Dike to affirm community as a desideratum in nature and society. Similarly, the claims of freedom are validated by what Hans Jonas so perceptively called the "inwardness" of life-forms, their "organic identity" and "adventure of form." The effort, venture, indeed self-recognition that every living being exercises in the course of "its precarious metabolic continuity" to preserve itself reveals—even in the most rudimentary of organisms—a sense of identity and selective activity that Jonas appropriately called evidence of "germinal freedom."[34]

"Open systems," "minds," and "holons" may explain the disequilibria that *change* cybernetic and general systems, but we must invariably fall back on inherent attributes of substance—notably, the motion, form, and *sensibilité* of "matter"—to account for the *development of nature toward complexity, specialization, and consciousness.* This necessity runs counter to every bias of current philosophy, which would ignore the fact of directiveness or endow it with human traits like *purposiveness* when it is simply a tendency that inheres in the organization of substance as potentiality.

*

The presuppositions I have made here are not arbitrary. The validity of a presupposition must be tested against the real *dialectic* of natural development—substance "free and self-moving in its own peculiar shape"—and not against the "atomies" of data and statistical probabilities adduced by empirical observation. On this score at least, contextualists like Whitehead and Bateson are quite sound in their claim that facts do not exist on their own but are always relational or *interactive*, to use Diderot's more germinal word.

Admittedly, this approach to a nature philosophy may seem as self-enclosed as the Kantian approach. But I have not faulted Kantian, neo-Kantian, or for that matter, cybernetic and positivistic theories for their internal unity or their impregnability to immanent criticism. My objection to them is their claim to universality, since their presuppositions provide an inadequate framework for understanding natural history and apprehending its ethical implications.

Finally, the study of nature exhibits a self-evolving *nisus,* so to speak, that is *implicitly* ethical. Mutualism, freedom, and subjectivity are not solely human values or concerns. They appear, *however germinally,* in larger cosmic or organic processes, but they require no Aristotelian God to motivate them, no Hegelian Spirit to vitalize them. If social ecology can provide a coherent focus on the unity of mutualism, freedom, and subjectivity as aspects of a cooperative society that is free of domination and guided by reflection and reason, it will have removed the difficulties that have plagued naturalistic ethics for so long. No longer would a Cartesian and Kantian dualism leave nature inert and mind isolated from the world around it. We would see that mind, far from being sui generis in a world that is wholly external to it, has a natural history that spans the *sensibilité* of the inorganic and the conceptual capacities of the human brain. To weaken community, to arrest the spontaneity of a self-organizing reality toward ever-greater complexity and rationality as nature rendered self-conscious, would be to deny our heritage in its evolutionary processes and dissolve our uniqueness in the world of life.

Mutualism, self-organization, freedom, and subjectivity, cohered by social ecology's principles of unity in diversity, spontaneity, and nonhierarchical relationships, are constitutive of evolution's potentialities. Aside from the ecological responsibilities they confer on our species as the self-reflexive voice of nature, they literally define us. Nature does not "exist" for us to use, but it makes possible our uniqueness. Like the concept of Being, these principles of social ecology require not analysis but merely verification. They are the elements of an ethical ontology, not rules of a game that can be changed to suit personal needs and interests.

NOTES

1. This article was written in September 1982 and published in 1985 in Michael Tobias, ed., *Deep Ecology* (San Diego, Calif.: Avant Books, 1985). It has been considerably revised for publication here.

2. For my distinction between environmentalism and ecology—more precisely, social ecology—see my "Toward an Ecological Society," initially delivered as a lecture at the University of Michigan, Ann Arbor, in the spring of 1973. It was published as an essay during the same year in *Roots* and *WIN* magazines and is now available as the leading essay in the collection of my 1970s writings, *Toward an Ecological Society* (Montreal: Black Rose Books, 1980).

3. This phrase is taken, of course, from Max Scheler's *Man's Place in Nature*.

4. Joseph Owens, foreword to Giovanni Reale, *The Concept of First Philosophy and the Unity of "The Metaphysics" of Aristotle* (Albany: State University of New York Press, 1980), p. xv.

5. See Martin Heidegger, *Early Greek Thinking*, trans. D. F. Krell and F. A. Capuzzi (New York: Harper and Row, 1975).

6. See Gregory Vlastos, "Equality and Justice in Early Greek Cosmologies," in *Studies in Presocratic Philosophy*, vol. 1, *The Beginnings of Philosophy*, ed. David J. Furley and R. E. Allen (London: Routledge and Kegan Paul; New York: Humanities Press, 1970), pp. 56-91.

7. Lawrence J. Henderson, *The Fitness of the Environment* (Boston: Beacon Press, 1958), pp. 1, 5.

8. Vlastos, "Equality and Justice," p. 60. Heraclitus, the least democratic of the Presocratics, does not speak of *isonomia* but of the "One," which we can properly distinguish from the "Whole." This mystical thrust already prefigures neo-Platonism, which would emphasize the transcendental and the socially elitist elements in Greek philosophy.

9. F. M. Cornford, *From Religion to Philosophy: A Study in the Origins of Western Speculation* (1912; New York: Harper and Row, 1957), p. 64.

10. *Ibid.*, p. 84.

11. *Ibid.*, p. 85.

12. Karl Jaspers, *Kant*, trans. Ralph Manheim (New York: Harcourt, Brace and World, 1962), pp. 50, 51.

13. A Kantian philosophy of subjectivity is certainly inadequate for social theory. To call for "intersubjectivity," for example, as in Jürgen Habermas's "ideal speech situation," without specifying what kind of political institutions are needed to give that "intersubjectivity" rational form, tells us little about the role of "intersubjectivity" in social relations. That Habermas himself, at this writing (1994), has turned to social

democracy as the best route to social rationality is evidence of the waywardness of "intersubjectivity" as a conceptual basis for social theory, analysis, and reconstruction.

14. G.W.F. Hegel, *The Philosophy of Mind*, trans. A. V. Miller (Oxford: The Clarendon Press, 1971), p. 315.

15. Gregory Bateson, *Mind and Nature: A Necessary Unity* (New York: E. P. Dutton, 1979), p. 11.

16. *Ibid.*, pp. 31, 93.

17. Arthur Koestler, *Janus: A Summing Up* (New York: Random House, 1978).

18. I have explored the mechanistic aspects of cybernetics and systems theory in "Energy, 'Ecotechnology,' and Ecology," in my *Toward an Ecological Society* (Montreal: Black Rose Books, 1980).

19. Morris Berman, an admirer of Bateson's work, has carefully explored the highly authoritarian character of Bateson's social outlook in *The Reenchantment of the World* (Ithaca, N.Y.: Cornell University Press, 1981), pp. 280-96. I disagree with Berman's view, however, that an anarchic ecological society follows from Bateson's cybernetic approach.

20. Koestler, *Janus*, pp. 30-34. Koestler tries to rescue the word *hierarchy* as an expression of "flexibility and freedom" in counterposition to reductionism, even as the term *hierarchy* haunts him because "it is loaded with military and ecclesiastical associations ... [and] conveys the impression of a rigid, authoritarian structure." I will certainly not dispute this latter view.

21. Bateson, *Mind and Nature*, p. 199.

22. Ludwig von Bertalanffy, *Robots, Men and Minds: Psychology in the Modern World* (New York: Braziller, 1967), p. 9.

23. *Ibid.*, pp. 69, 71.

24. Gregoire Nicolis and Ilya Prigogine, *Self-Organization in Nonequilibrium Systems* (New York: John Wiley, 1977). For more on Prigoginian systems theory, see my essay "Thinking Ecologically," elsewhere in this book.

25. By far the best English translation of Diderot's works is Jean Stewart and Jonathan Kemp's *Diderot: Interpreter of Nature: Selected Writings* (New York: International Publishers, 1936), which captures the elegance and rich nuance of Diderot's prose that are often lost in English translations.

26. G.W.F. Hegel, *Phenomenology of Spirit*, trans. A. V. Miller (Oxford: The Clarendon Press, 1977), p. 49.

27. Friedrich Engels, *Feuerbach and the End of Classical German Philosophy*, in Marx and Engels, *Selected Works*, vol. 2, p. 330; quoted in Georg Lukács, *The Young Hegel: Studies in the Relations between Dialectics and Economics*, trans. Rodney Livingstone (Cambridge, Mass.: MIT Press; London: The Merlin Press, 1975), p. 468.

28. See Erwin Schrödinger, *What is Life? Mind and Matter* (Garden City, N.Y.: Doubleday, 1956). For a more detailed account of the new advances in astrophysics and biology, see my *The Ecology of Freedom* (1982; Montreal: Black Rose Books, 1990), from which a number of these passages, generally in modified form, are drawn.

29. William Trager, *Symbiosis* (New York: Van Nostrand Reinhold, 1970), p. vii.

30. Lynn Margulis, *Symbiosis in Cell Evolution* (San Francisco: W. H. Freeman, 1981). My citation of Margulis applies only to her notion that life played a role in creating the biosphere. It should not be taken as endorsing either her reductionist views of prokaryotic cells or her acceptance of the mystical Gaia Hypothesis.

31. Manfred Eigen, "Molecular Self-Organization and the Early Stages of Evolution," *Quarterly Review of Biophysics*, vol. 4 (1971), p. 202.

32. Margulis, *Symbiosis*, pp. 348-49.

33. Elizabeth Vrba cited in Robert Lewin, "Evolutionary Theory Under Fire," *Science*, vol. 210 (1980), pp. 885.

34. Hans Jonas, *The Phenomenon of Life* (New York: Delta, 1966), pp. 82, 90.

FREEDOM AND NECESSITY IN NATURE
A Problem in Ecological Ethics[1]

One of the most entrenched ideas in Western thought is the notion that nature is a harsh realm of necessity, a domain of unrelenting lawfulness and compulsion. From this underlying idea, two extreme attitudes have emerged. Either humanity must yield with religious or "ecological" humility to the dicta of "natural law" and take its abject place side by side with the lowly ants on which it "arrogantly" treads, *or* it must "conquer" nature by means of its technological and rational astuteness, in a shared project ultimately to "liberate" all of humanity from the compulsion of natural "necessity"—an enterprise that may well entail the subjugation of human by human.

The first attitude, a quasi-religious quietism, is typified by "deep ecology," antihumanism, and sociobiology, while the second, an activist approach, is typified by the liberal and Marxian image of an omniscient humanity cast in a commandeering posture toward the natural world. Modern science—despite its claims to value-free objectivity—unwittingly takes on an ethical mantle when it commits itself to a concept of nature as comprehensible, as orderly in the sense that nature's "laws" are rationally explicable and basically necessitarian.

The ancient Greeks viewed this orderly structure of the natural world as evidence of a cosmic *nous* or *logos* that produced a subjective presence in natural phenomena as a whole. Yet with only a minimal shift in emphasis, this same notion of an orderly nature can yield the dismal conclusion that "freedom is the recognition of necessity" (to use Friedrich Engels's rephrasing of Hegel's definition). In this latter case, freedom is subtly turned into its opposite: the mere *consciousness* of what we can or cannot do.

Such an internalized view of freedom as subject to higher dicta, of "Spirit" (Hegel) or "History" (Marx), not only served Luther in his break with the Church's hierarchy; it provided an ideological justification for Stalin's worst excesses in the name of dialectical materialism and his brutal industrialization of Russia under the aegis of society's "natural laws of development." It may also yield an outright Skinnerian notion of an overly determined world in which human behavior is reduced to mere responses to external or internal stimuli.

These extremes aside, the conventional wisdom of our time still sees nature as a harsh "realm of necessity"—morally, as well as materially—that constitutes a challenge to humanity's survival and well-being, not to speak of its freedom. With the considerable intellectual heritage of dystopian thinkers like Hobbes and utopian ones like Marx, the self-definition of major academic disciplines embodies this tension, indeed, this conflict. Economics was forged in the crucible of a necessitarian, even "stingy" nature whose "scarce resources" were thought to be insufficient to meet humanity's "unlimited needs." Psychology, certainly in its psychoanalytic forms, stresses the importance of controlling human internal nature, with the bonus that the individual's sublimated energy will find its expression in the subjugation of external nature. Theories of work, society, behavior, and even sexuality turn on an image of a necessitarian nature that must in some sense be "dominated" to serve human ends—presumably on the old belief that what is natural disallows *all* elements of choice and freedom. Nor is nature philosophy itself untainted by this harshly necessitarian image. Indeed, more often than not, it has served as an ideological justification for a hierarchical society, modeled on a hierarchically structured "natural order."

This image and its social implications, generally associated with Aristotle, still live in our midst as a cosmic justification for domination in general—in its more noxious cases, for racial and sexual discrimination, and in its most nightmarish form, for the outright extermination of entire peoples. Raised to a moral calling, "man" emerges from this massive ideological apparatus as a creature to whom "Spirit" or "God" has imparted a supranatural quality of a transcendental kind and a mission to govern an ordered universe that "He" or "It" created.

*

At first glance, resolving the conflict between necessity and freedom—presumably between nature and society—seems to require building a bridge between the two, as in value systems that are based on purely utilitarian attitudes toward the natural world. The argument that humanity's abuse of nature subverts the material conditions for our own survival, although surely true, is nonetheless crassly instrumental. It assumes that human concern for nature rests on self-interest rather than on a feeling for the living world of which human beings are part, albeit in a very distinctive way. In such a value system our relationship with nature is neither better nor worse than the success with which we plunder it without harming ourselves. It is another warrant for undermining the natural world, provided only that we can find adequate substitutes, however synthetic, simple, or mechanical, for existing life-forms and ecological relationships. It is precisely this approach that has exacerbated the present ecological crisis.

Moreover, attempts to bridge the gulf between the natural and social worlds that are premised on a mechanical dualism between nature and society can indirectly preserve this dualism even as they seek to overcome it. This kind of purely *structural* approach has given rise to splits between body and mind, reality and thought, object and subject, country and town, and ultimately, society and the individual. It is not far-fetched to say that the primary schism between nature and humanity has nourished a wide variety of splits in everyday life as well as in our theoretical sensibilities.

No less serious a fallacy is to attempt to overcome these dualisms simply by reducing one element of the duality to the other or, seriously, to attempt to dissolve humanity into nature. The universal "night in which all cows are black," as Hegel phrased it in his *Phenomenology of Spirit*, attains unity by sacrificing the variety and the uniqueness of humanity as a remarkable product of natural evolution. Such reductionism yields a crude mechanistic spiritualism that is merely the counterpart of the prevailing mechanistic materialism. In either case, a nuanced interpretation of evolutionary phenomena that takes into account distinctions and gradations as well as continuities is replaced by a simplistic dualism that dismisses the phases that enter into any process. It embraces a simplistic and mystical "Oneness" that overrides the immense wealth of differentiae to which the present biosphere is heir—the rich, fecund constituents that make up our evolution and that are preserved in nearly all existing phenomena.

It is surprising that ecology, one of the most organic of contemporary disciplines, is itself so lacking in organic ways of thinking—that is, in forms of reason that inwardly derive, or educe, differentiae from one another, the full from the germinal, the complex from the simple—in short, in thinking organically and eductively, not merely deducing conclusions from hypotheses in typical mathematical fashion, or simply tabulating and classifying facts. Ecologists too often share with accountants the mode of reasoning so prevalent today, one that is largely analytical and classificatory rather than processual and developmental. Appropriate as analytical, classificatory, and deductive modes of reasoning are for assembling automobile engines or constructing buildings, they are woefully inadequate for ascertaining the phases that make up a process, each with its own integrity yet as part of an ever-developing continuum. We may well fail to understand life itself if we see life-forms as little more than factors in production, as "natural resources" to be placed in the service of wealth, rather than as part of the creative phenomenon of life. Again, this mechanistic sensibility and its analytic mode of thought is alien to processual thought, to apprehending development and its phases—both their differences and their continuities.

It is becoming a cliché to fault humanity's "separation" from nature as the source of "alienation" in our highly fragmented world. We must see that *every* process is also a form of alienation, in the sense that differentiation involves separation from older forms of being as well as the absorption of what is negated into the new, such that the whole is the richly varied fulfillment of its latent potentialities. Standing in marked contrast to this view of alienation as self-expression or self-articulation as well as opposition is an all-pervasive epistemology of rule that sorts difference as such (indeed, the "other" in all its forms) into an ensemble of antagonistic relationships structured around command and obedience. That the "other" is at least part of a whole, however differentiated it is, eludes the modern mind in a flux of experience that knows division exclusively as conflict or breakdown.[2]

The real world is indeed divided antagonistically, to be remedied by struggle, reconciliation—and transcendence. But if the thrust of evolution has any meaning, it is that a continuum is processual precisely in that it is graded as well as united, a flow of derived phases as well as a shared development from the simpler to the more complex. Neither conflict nor differentiation should be permitted to override the other as the long-range character of development in nature and society.

*

What then does it mean to speak of complexity, variety, and unity-in-diversity in developmental processes? Ecologists generally treat diversity as a source of ecological stability, in the belief that while the vulnerability to pests of a single crop treated with pesticides can reach alarming proportions, a more diversified crop, in which a number of plant and animal species interact, produces natural checks on pest populations.[3]

But the fact that biotic—and social—evolution has been marked until recently by the development of ever more complex species and ecocommunities raises an even more challenging issue. The diversity of an ecocommunity may be a source of greater stability from an agricultural standpoint; but from an evolutionary standpoint, it may be an ever-expanding, albeit nascent source of freedom within nature, a medium for providing varying degrees of *choice, self-directiveness, and participation by life-forms in their own development.*

I wish to propose that the evolution of living beings is no mere passive process, the product of exclusively chance conjunctions between random genetic changes and "selective" environmental "forces," and that the "origin of species" is no mere result of external influences that determine the "fitness" of a life-form to "survive" as a result of random factors in which life is simply an "object" of an indeterminable "selective" process. The increase in diversity in the biosphere *opens new evolutionary pathways,* indeed, alternative evolutionary directions, in which species play an *active* role in their own survival and change. However nascent, choice is not totally absent from biotic evolution; indeed, it increases as species become structurally, physiologically, and above all neurologically more complex. As the ecological contexts within which species evolve—the communities and interactions they form—become more complex, they open new avenues for evolution and a greater ability of life-forms to act self-selectively, forming the bases for some kind of choice, favoring precisely those species that can participate in ever-greater degrees in their own evolution, basically in the direction of greater complexity. Indeed, species and the ecocommunities in which they interact to create more complex forms of evolutionary development are increasingly the very "forces" that account for evolution as a whole.

"Participatory evolution," as I call this view, is somewhat at odds with the prevalent Darwinian or neo-Darwinian syntheses, in which nonhuman life-forms are primarily "objects" of selective forces exogenous to them. No less is it at odds with Henri Bergson's "creative evolution," with its semimystical *élan vital.* Ecologists, like biologists, have yet to come to terms with the notion that symbiosis (not only "struggle") and participation (not only "competition") factor in the evolution of species. The prevalent view of nature still stresses the exclusively "necessitarian" character of the natural world. An immense literature, both artistic and scientific, stresses the "cruelty" of a nature that bears no witness to the suffering of life and that is "indifferent" to cries of pain in the "struggle for existence." "Cruel" nature, in this imagery, offers no solace for extinction—merely an all-embracing darkness of meaningless motion to which humanity can oppose only the light of its culture and mind. Such formulations impart a sophisticated ethical dimension to the natural world that is more anthropomorphic than meaningful.

But even if the formulation is anthropomorphic, it bespeaks a presence in natural evolution—subjectivity and specifically *human* consciousness—that cannot be ignored in formulating an evolutionary theory. We may reasonably claim that human will and freedom, at least as self-consciousness and self-reflection, have their own natural history in potentialities of the natural world—in contrast to the view that they are sui generis, the product of a rupture with the whole of development so unprecedented and unique that it contradicts the gradedness of all phenomena from the antecedent potentialities that lie behind and within every processual "product." Such claims are intended to underwrite our efforts to deal with the natural world as we choose—indeed, as Marx put it in the *Grundrisse,* to regard nature merely as "an object for mankind, purely a matter of utility."

The dim choices that animals exercise in their own evolution should not be confused with the will and degree of intentionality that human beings exhibit in their social lives. Nor is the nascent freedom that is rendered possible by natural complexity comparable to the ability of humans to make rational decisions. The differences between the two are qualitative, however much they can be traced back to the evolution of all animals.

Our tendency to ignore the close interaction between evolving life-forms and the environmental forces that "select" them for survival is a mechanistic prejudice that still clings to evolutionary theory. All anti-Cartesian protestations to the contrary, we still view nonhuman life-forms as little more than machines or inert beings. Structurally, we may fill them out with protoplasm, but operationally we impute no more meaning to them than to mechanical devices—a judgment, it is worth noting, that is not without economic utility in dealing with working people as "hands" or "operatives."

Despite the monumental nature of his work, Darwin did not fully organicize evolutionary theory. He brought a profound evolutionary sensibility to the "origin of species," but in the minds of his acolytes species still stood somewhere between inorganic machines and mechanically functioning organisms. No less significant are the empirical origins of Darwin's own work, which are deeply rooted in the Lockean atomism that nourished nineteenth-century British science as a whole. Allowing for the nuances that appear in all great books, *The Origin of Species* accounts for the way in which *individual* species originate, evolve, adapt, survive, change, or pay the penalty of extinction as if they were fairly isolated from their environment. In that account, any one species stands for the world of life as a whole, in isolation from the life-forms that normally interact with it and with which it is interdependent. Although predators depend upon their prey, to be sure, Darwin portrays the strand from ancestor to descendant in lofty isolation, such that early *eohippus* rises, step by step, from its plebeian estate to attain the aristocratic grandeur of a sleek race horse. The paleontological diagramming of bones from former "missing links" to the culminating beauty of *Equus caballus* more closely resembles the adaptation of Robinson Crusoe from an English seafarer to a self-sufficient island dweller than the reality of a truly emerging being.

This reality is contextual in an ecological sense. The horse lived not only among its predators and food but in creatively interactive relationships with a great variety of plants and animals. It evolved not alone but in ever-changing ecocommunities, such that the "rise" of *Equus caballus* occurred conjointly with that of other herbivores that shared and maintained their grasslands and even played a major role in creating them. The string of bones that traces *eohippus* to *Equus* is evidence of the succession of ecocommunities in which the ancestral animal and its descendants interacted with other life-forms.

One could more properly modify *The Origin of Species* to read as the evolution of ecocommunities as well as the evolution of species.[4] Indeed, placing the community in the foreground of evolution does not deny the integrity of species, their capacity for variation, or their unique lines of development. Species become vital participants in their own evolution—active beings, not merely passive components—taking full account of their nascent freedom in the natural process.

Nor are will and reason sui generis. They have their origins in the growing choices conferred by complexity and in the alternative pathways opened up by the growth of complex ecocommunities and the development of increasingly complex neurological systems—in short, processes that are both internal and external to life-forms. To speak of evolution in very broad terms tends to conceal the specific evolutionary *processes* that make up the overall process. Many anatomical lines of evolution have occurred: the evolution of the various organs that freed life-forms from their aquatic milieu; of eyes and ears, which sophisticated their awareness of the surrounding environment; and of the nervous system, from nerve networks to brains. Thus, mind too has its evolutionary history in the natural world, and as the neurological capability of life-forms to function more actively and flexibly increases, so too does life itself help create new evolutionary directions that lead to enhanced self-awareness and self-activity. Selfhood appears germinally in the communities that life-forms establish as *active agents in their own evolution,* contrary to conventional evolutionary theory.

*

Does the nature of evolution warrant introducing a presiding agent into evolutionary and ecological theory, one that predetermines the development of life-forms along the lines I have described, a "Spirit," "God," "Mind," or perhaps a semimystical Bergsonian *élan vital*? I think not, if only because the concept of such a hidden hand preserves the nature-society dualism itself. So profoundly does dualism inhere in our mental operations that when we consider the immanent striving of life-forms toward various degrees of freedom and self-awareness, we often slip into explanations involving supernature rather than nature itself, reductionism rather than differentiation, and succession rather than culmination. Hence the present revival of the "reverence for nature" that the nineteenth-century Romantic tradition so poetically cultivated, a "revered" natural world dissolved into a mystical "oneness."

Not only does this "reverence" preserve and even foster a nature-society dualism; it restores to evolutionary theory the very dualism that underpins hierarchy and the view of all differentiation as degrees of domination and subordination. A "revered" nature is a separated nature in the bad sense of the term—that is to say, a mystified nature. Like the deities that human beings create in their imagination and worship in temples, mediated by priests and gurus with their incantations and rituals, this separated nature becomes a reified and contrived phenomenon that is set apart from the human world, even as human beings genuflect before a mystified "It." "Reverence" for nature, the mythologizing of the natural world, degrades it by denying nature its universality as that which exists everywhere, free of dualities like "Spirit" and "God."

If liberal and Marxist theorists prepared the ideological bases for plundering the natural world, "biocentrically" oriented antihumanists and "natural law" devotees may be preparing the ideological bases for plundering the human spirit. In the course of "revering nature," they have created an insidious image of a humanity whose "intrinsic worth" is no more or less than that of other species. "Biocentrism" denies humanity its real place in natural evolution by completely subordinating humanity to the natural world. Paradoxically, "biocentrism" and antihumanism also contribute to the alienation and reification of nature such that a "reverence" for nature can easily be used to negate any existential respect for the diversity of life. Against the background of a cosmic "Nature," human life and individuality are completely trivialized, as witness James Lovelock's description of people as merely "intelligent fleas" feeding on the body of Gaia. Nor can we ignore a growing number of "natural law" acolytes who advocate authoritarian measures to control population growth and forcibly expel urban dwellers from large congested cities, as though a society that is structured around the domination of human by human could be expected to leave the natural world intact.

It is grossly misleading to invoke "biocentrism," "natural law," and antihumanism for ends that deny the most distinctive of human natural attributes: the ability to reason, to foresee, to will, and to act insightfully to enhance nature's own development. In a sense, it deprecates nature to separate these subjective attributes from it, as though they did not emerge out of evolutionary development and were not implicitly part of animal development. A humanity that has been rendered oblivious to its own responsibility to evolution—a responsibility to bring reason and the human spirit to evolutionary development, to foster diversity, and to provide ecological guidance such that the harmful and the fortuitous in the natural world are diminished—is a humanity that *betrays its own evolutionary heritage* and that ignores its species-distinctiveness and uniqueness.

Ironically, then, a nature that is reverentially hypostatized is a nature set apart from humanity—and in the very process of being hypostatized over humanity, it is defamed. A nature reconstructed into forms apart from itself, however "reverential-ly," easily becomes a mere object of utility. Indeed, a revered nature is the converse of the old liberal and Marxian image of nature "dominated" by man. Both attitudes reinstate the theme of domination in ecological discussion.

Here the limited form of reasoning based on *deduction*, so commonplace in conventional logic, supplants an organismic form of reasoning based on *eduction*—that is, on derivation, so deeply rooted in the dialectical outlook. *Potentially*, human reason is an expression of nature rendered self-conscious, a nature that finds its voice in being of its own creation. It is not only we who must have our own place in nature but nature that must have its place in us—in an ecological society and in an ecological ethics based on humanity's catalytic role in natural evolution.

*

Along with the antihumanistic ideologies that foster mis-anthropic attitudes and actions, the reduction of human beings to commodities is steadily denaturing and degrading humanity. The commodification of humanity takes its most pernicious form in the manipulation of the individual as a means of production and consumption. Here, human beings are employed (in the literal sense of the term) as techniques either in production or in consumption, as mere devices whose creative powers and authentic needs are equally perverted into objectified phenomena. As a result, we are witnessing today not only the "fetishization of commodities" (to use Marx's famous formulation) but the fetishization of needs.[5] Human beings are becoming separated from their own nature as well as from the natural world in an existential split that threatens to give dramatic reality to Descartes's theoretical split between the soul and the body. In this sense, the claim that capitalism is a totally "unnatural order" is only too accurate.

The terrible tragedy of the present social era is not only that it is polluting the environment; it is also simplifying natural ecocommunities, social relationships, *and even the human psyche.* The pulverization of the natural world is being accompanied by the pulverization of the social and psychological worlds. In this sense, the conversion of soil into sand in agriculture can be said, in a metaphorical sense, to apply to society and the human spirit. The greatest danger we face—apart from nuclear immolation—is the homogenization of the world by a market society and its objectification of all human relationships and experiences into commodities.

To recover human nature is not only to recover its continuity with the creative process of natural evolution but to recognize its distinctiveness. To conceive of the participation of life-forms in evolution is to understand that nature is a realm of incipient freedom. It is freedom and participation—not simply necessity—that we must emphasize, an emphasis that involves a radical break with the conventional image of nature.

Social ecology, in effect, stands at odds with the notion that culture has no roots whatever in natural evolution. Indeed, it explores the roots of the cultural in the natural and seeks to ascertain the gradations of biological development that phase the natural into the social. By the same token, it also tries to explore the important differences that distinguish the societal from the natural and to ascertain the gradations of social development that, hopefully, will yield a new, humanistic ecological society. The two lines of exploration go together in producing a larger whole, indeed, one that must transcend even the present capitalist society based on perpetual growth and profit. To identify society as such with the *present* society, to see in capitalism an "emancipatory" movement precisely because it frees us from nature, is not only to ignore the roots of society in nature but to identify a perverted society with humanism and thereby to give credence to the antihumanist trends in ecological thinking.

This much is clear: the way we view our position in the natural world is deeply entangled with the way we organize the social world. In large part, the former derives from the latter and serves, in turn, to reinforce social ideology. Every society projects its own perception of itself onto nature, whether as a tribal cosmos that is rooted in kinship communities, a feudal cosmos that originates in and underpins a strict hierarchy of rights and duties, a bourgeois cosmos structured around a market society that fosters human rivalry and competition, or a corporate cosmos diagrammed in flow charts, feedback systems, and hierarchies that mirror the operational systems of modern corporate society. That some of these images reveal a truthful aspect of nature, whether as a community or a cybernetic flow of energy, does not justify the universal, almost imperialistic claims that their proponents stake out for them over the world as a whole. Ultimately, only a society that has come into its "truth," to use

Hegelian language—a rational and ecological society—can free us from the limits that oppressive and hierarchical societies impose on our understanding of nature.

The power of social ecology lies in the association it establishes between society and ecology, in understanding that the social is, potentially at least, a fulfillment of the *latent* dimension of freedom in nature, and that the ecological is a major organizing principle of social development. In short, social ecology advances the guidelines for an ecological society. The great divorce between nature and society—or between the "biological" and the "cultural"—is overcome by shared developmental concepts such as greater diversity in evolution; the wider and more complete participation of all components in a whole; and the ever more fecund potentialities that expand the horizon of freedom and self-reflexivity. Society, like mind, ceases to be sui generis. Like mind, with its natural history, social life emerges from the loosely banded animal community to form the highly institutionalized human community.[6]

Social ecology challenges the image of an unmediated natural evolution, in which the human mind, society, and even culture are sui generis, in which nonhuman nature is irretrievably separated from human nature, and in which an ethically defamed nature finds no expression whatever in society, mind, and human will. It seeks to throw a critical and meaningful light on the phased, graded, and cumulative development of nature into society, richly mediated by the prolonged dependence of the human young on parental care, by the blood tie as the earliest social and cultural bond beyond immediate parental care, by the so-called "sexual division of labor," and by age-based status groups and their role in the origin of hierarchy.

Ultimately, it is the institutionalization of the human community that distinguishes society from the nonhuman community—whether for the worse, as in the case of pre-1789 France or tsarist Russia, where weak, unfeeling tyrants like Louis XVI and Nicholas II were raised to commanding positions by bureaucracies, armies, and social classes; or for the better, as in forms of self-governance and management that empower the people as a whole, like the Parisian sections during the French Revolution and the anarchosyndicalist collectives during the Spanish Civil War. We see no such contrived institutional infrastructures in nonhuman communities, although the rudiments of a social bond do exist in the mother-offspring relationship and in common forms of mutual aid.

With a growing knowledge that sharing, cooperation, and concern foster healthy human consociation, with the technical disciplines that open the way for a creative "metabolism" between humanity and nature, and with a host of new insights into the presence of nature in so much of our own civilization, it can no longer be denied that nature is still with us. Indeed, it has returned to us ideologically as a challenge to the devouring of "natural resources" for profit and the mindless simplification of the biosphere. We can no longer speak meaningfully of a "new" or "rational" society without also tailoring our social relationships and institutions to the ecocommunities in which our social communities are located. In short, any rational future society must be an ecological society, conjoining humanity's capacity for innovation, technological development, and intellectuality with the nonhuman natural world on which civilization itself rests and human well-being depends.

The ecological principles that enter into biotic evolution do not disappear from social evolution, any more than the natural history of mind can be dissolved into Kant's ahistorical epistemology. Quite the contrary: the societal and cultural are ecologically derivative, as the men's and women's houses in tribal communities so clearly illustrate. The relationship between nature and society is a cumulative one, while each remains distinctive and creative in its own right. Perhaps most significant, the nature of which the societal and cultural are derivative—and cumulative—is a nature that is a potential realm of freedom and subjectivity, and humanity is potentially the most self-conscious and self-reflexive expression of that natural development.

*

Social ecology, by definition, takes on the responsibility of evoking, elaborating, and giving an ethical content to the natural core of society and humanity.[7] Granting the limitations that society imposes on our thinking, the development of mind out of "first nature" produces an objective ground for an ethics, indeed, for formulating a vision of a rational society that is neither hierarchical nor relativistic: an ethics that is based neither on atavistic appeals to "blood and soil" and inexorable "social laws" ("dialectical" or "scientific") on the one hand, nor on the wayward consensus of public opinion polls, which will support capital punishment one year and life imprisonment the next. Freedom becomes a desideratum as self-reflexivity, as self-management, and most excitingly, as a creative and active process that, *with its ever-expanding horizon,* resists the moral imperatives of a rigid definition and the jargon of temporally conditioned biases.[8]

An ecological ethics of freedom would provide an objective directiveness to the human enterprise. We have no need to degrade nature or society into a crude biologism at one extreme or a crude dualism at the other. A diversity that nurtures freedom, an interactivity that enhances complementarity, a wholeness that fosters creativity, a community that strengthens individuality, a growing subjectivity that yields greater rationality—all are desiderata that provide the ground for an objective ethics. They are also the real principles of any graded evolution, one that renders not only the past explicable but the future meaningful.

An ecological ethics of freedom cannot be divorced from a technics that enhances our relationship with nature—a creative, not destructive, "metabolism" with nature. Human beings must be active agents in the biosphere—vividly, expressively, and rationally—not retreat into the passive animism of pagan, Taoist, and Buddhist mystics who recycle Asian philosophies and sensibilities through the ashrams and religious temples of the Pacific rim of the United States. But it makes all the difference in the world if we cultivate food not only on behalf of our physical well-being but with regard for the well-being of the soil as well. Inasmuch as agriculture is always a culture, the differences in the methods and intentions involved are no less cultural than a book on engineering. Yet in the first case, our intentions are informed by economic considerations at best and greed at worst; in the second, by an ecological sensibility. Society must recover the plasticity of the organic in the sense that every dimension of experience must be infused with an ecological, a *dialectical* sensibility. There is a profoundly ethical dimension to the attempt to bring soil, flora, and fauna (or what we neatly call the food chain) into our lives, not only as "wholesome" sources of food but as part of a broad movement in which consumption is no less a creative process than production—originating in the soil and returning to it in a richer form all the components that make up the food cycle.

So, too, in the production of objects it makes all the difference in the world if craftspeople work with a respect for their materials, emphasizing quality and artistry in production rather than mass-producing commodities with no concern for handling materials sparingly, let alone for human needs. In the former, production and consumption go beyond the pure economic domain of the buyer-seller relationship, indeed, beyond the domain of mere material sustenance, and enter into the ecological domain as a mode of enhancing the fecundity of an eco-community. An ecotechnology—for consumption no less than production—serves to enrich an ecosystem just as compost in food cultivation enriches the soil, rather than degrading and simplifying the natural fundament of life. An ecotechnology is thus a moral technology, a technology that stands at odds with gigantism, waste, and the mass destruction wrought on the environment by capitalistic forms of technology designed purely for profit.

The choices we make in these respects—in the food we grow and eat, in the objects we produce and consume—are between an ecological alternative and a purely economic one. We are profoundly influenced by social institutions, whichever alternative we choose. In the end, our choice will be between an ecocommunity or a market community, between a society infused by life or a society infused by gain. Yet no rational society can hope to exist, still less stabilize itself, without amply meeting human needs and providing the free time to create a fully democratic polity. The advances in technology that mark the past few centuries cannot be dismissed exclusively because of the damage they have inflicted both on the natural world and on the human condition. For now we can at least *choose* the kind of world in which we want to live—we can choose to bring science and technological knowledge to the service of humanity and the biosphere alike.

To say that nature belongs in humanity just as humanity belongs in nature is to express a highly reciprocal and complementary relationship between the two instead of one structured around subordination and domination. Neither society nor nature dissolves into the other. Rather, social ecology tries to recover the distinctive attributes of both in a continuum that gives rise to a substantive ethics, wedding the social to the ecological without denying the integrity of each.

*

The fecundity and potentiality for freedom that variety and complexity bring to natural evolution, indeed, that emerge from natural evolution, can also be said in a qualitatively advanced form to apply to social evolution and psychic development. The more diversified a society and its psychic life, the more creative it is, and the greater the opportunity for freedom it is likely to offer—not only in terms of new choices that open up to human beings but also in terms of the richer social background that diversity and complexity create. As in natural evolution, so too in social evolution we must go beyond the image that diversity and complexity yield greater stability—the usual claim that ecologists make for the two—and emphasize that they yield greater creativity, choices, and freedom.

At the same time there can be no return to the past—to the domestic realm, to the age-ranks, or to the kinship relationships of tribalism. Nor can there be a return to the myths, amulets, magical practices, and idols—female or male—of the past. While we redeem what is valuable in premodern societies for enhancing human solidarity and an ecological sensibility, we must also transcend all the parochial and divisive features of the past and present. If we are to create a truly rational and ecological society, we must nourish the insights provided by reason to create a sense of a shared humanity that is bound neither by gendered outlooks nor by beliefs in deities—all of which, ironically, are merely anthropomorphic projections of our own beings and sensibilities (as Ludwig Feuerbach so clearly saw)—and we must commit ourselves to a belief in the potentialities of humanity to foresee and understand, to be the embodiment of mind.

No ecological ethics of freedom can be divorced from a politics of participation, a politics that fosters self-empowerment rather than state empowerment. Such a politics must become a truly peopled politics in the sense that political participation is literally peopled by assemblies and by face-to-face discussion. The political ethics that follows from this ground is meant to create an ethical community, not simply an "efficient" one; an ecological community, not simply an environmentally "hygienic" one; a social and political praxis that yields freedom, not a statist culture that merely allows a measure of public assent.

If history is a bloody "slaughterbench," the blood that covers it is not only that of civilization's innocent victims but that of the angry men and women who have left us a legacy of freedom. The legacy of freedom and the legacy of domination have often been tragically intermingled. If we are to rescue ourselves from the homogenizing effects of a market society, it is necessary that humanity's waning memory of heroic struggles to achieve freedom be rescued from this society's pollution—a process that has already gone far in contemporary culture.

NOTES

1. This article was originally published in *Alternatives,* vol. 13, no. 4 (November 1986). It has been significantly revised for publication here.
2. Despite some recent nonsense to the effect that the Frankfurt School reconnoitered a nonhierarchical and ecological view of society's future, in no sense were its ablest thinkers, Max Horkheimer and Theodor Adorno, resolutely critical of hierarchy and domination. Rather, their views were clearly pessimistic: reason and civilization, for better or worse, entail "uncompromising individuals [who] may have been in favor of unity and cooperation ... to build a strong hierarchy. ... The history of the old religions and schools like that of the modern parties and revolutions teaches us that the price for survival is practical involvement, the transformation of ideas into domination." See Horkheimer and Adorno, *Dialectic of Enlightenment* (New York: Herder and Herder, 1972; originally published in 1944), pp. 213, 215. The power of these thinkers lay in their opposition to positivism and the theoretical problems they raised, not in the solutions they offered. Attempts to make them into proto-social ecologists, much less precursors of bioregionalism, involve a gross misreading of their ideas or, worse, a failure to read their works at all.
3. This approach was still rather new some twenty-five years ago, when I pioneered it together with rare colleagues like Charles S. Elton. Today it has become commonplace in ecological and environmental thinking, as have organic methods of gardening.
4. Darwin did not deny the role of animal interactivity in evolution, particularly in the famous Chapter 3 of *The Origin of Species,* where he suggests that "ever-increasing circles of complexity" check populations that, left uncontrolled, would reach pest proportions. But he sees this as a "battle within battles [which] must be continually recurring with varying success" (on p. 58 of the Modern Library edition). Moreover, "the dependency of one organic being on another"—typically "as of a parasite on its prey"—is secondary to the struggle "between individuals of the same species" (p. 60). Like most Victorians, Darwin had a strongly providential and moral side to his character: "we may console ourselves," he assures us, "that the war of nature is generally prompt, and that the vigorous, the healthy, and the happy survive and multiply" (p. 62). Indeed: "How fleeting are the wishes and efforts of man! how short his time! and consequently how poor will be his results, compared with those accumulated by Nature's productions during whole geological periods! Can we wonder, then, that Nature's productions should be far 'truer' than man's productions; that they should be infinitely better

adapted to the most complex conditions of life, and should plainly bear the stamp of a far higher workmanship?" (p. 66). These remarks do not make Darwin an ecologist but are marvelous asides to a thesis that emphasizes variation, selection, fitness, and above all struggle. Yet one cannot help but be entranced by a moral sensibility that would have been magnificently responsive to the message of modern ecology and that deserves none of the onerous rubbish that has been imputed to the man because of social Darwinism.

5. See Murray Bookchin, *The Ecology of Freedom* (Palo Alto: Cheshire Books, 1982; Montreal: Black Rose Books, 1991), pp. 68-69.

6. An ecological approach can spare us some of the worst absurdities of sociobiology and biological reductionism. The popular notion that our deep-seated "reptilian" brain is responsible for our aggressive, "brutish," and cruel behavioral traits may make for good television dramas like *Cosmos*, but it is ridiculous science. Like all the great animal groups, most Mesozoic reptiles were almost certainly gentle herbivores, not carnivores—and those that were carnivores were probably neither more nor less aggressive, "brutish," or "cruel" than mammals. Our images of Tyrannosaurus rex (a creature whose generic name is sociological nonsense) may be inordinately frightening, but they grossly distort the reptilian life-forms on which the carnivore preyed. If anything, the majority of Mesozoic reptiles were probably very pacific and easily frightened, all the more because they were not particularly intelligent vertebrates. What remains unacknowledged in this imagery of fierce, fire-breathing, and "unfeelingly cruel" reptiles is the implicit assumption of different psychic sensibilities in reptiles and mammals, the latter presumably being more "sensitive" and "understanding" than the former. A psychic evolution in nonhuman beings thus goes together with the evolution of intelligence. Yet confronted with the unstated premises of such evolutionary trends, few scientists would find them comfortable.

7. This project is elaborated in considerable detail in my book *The Ecology of Freedom.*

8. Hence freedom is no longer resolvable into a strident nihilistic negativity or a trite instrumental positivity. Rather, in its open-endedness, it contains both and transcends them as a continuing process. Freedom thus resists precise definition just as it resists terminal finality. It is always becoming, hopefully surpassing what it was in the past and developing into what it can be in the future.

THINKING ECOLOGICALLY
A Dialectical Approach[1]

In a time of sweeping social breakdown and intellectual fragmentation, it is not surprising to find that patchwork eclecticism and ideological faddism are seriously corroding the very notion of coherent thinking. Although such ideological deterioration has occurred in earlier periods of social decay, one might have hoped that ecological thinking—with its emphasis on the organic, the holistic, and the developmental—would have provided an ideological terrain from which we could resist the general fragmentation of our times. Tragically, this hope has not been fulfilled. Many contemporary ecophilosophies, in fact, far from countering the trend toward eclecticism and faddism, seem to be reinforcing it. Indeed, we are being overwhelmed by an effluvium of fads prefixed by *eco-* that pander to New Age pop styles. Too often, these "eco"-faddists either ignore muscularity of thought as too "heavy," or else they condemn it as intellectually "linear" and "divisive." As a result, a mentally lazy readership is emerging that is startled by serious thought that is in any way demanding—and even "turned off" by it (to use "counterculture" jargon).

More specifically, Taoist moods, Buddhist homilies, and New Age platitudes seem to be replacing even genuine thinking, let alone the possibility of organic reasoning that social ecology raised a decade or so ago. As simplified interpretations of Eastern thought—light-mindedly mixed with Heideggerian "woodpaths" and Jungian archetypes—obscure the many gnawing philosophical problems that are endemic to ecological thought, surprisingly few ecologically oriented people seem to feel that Western philosophy and social theory have much to contribute. Instead, the Western tradition is reviled as the monolithic source of ecological problems. Indeed, it is stylish to heap epithets on Descartes as the "source" of dualism and on Francis Bacon as the "source" of scientism—with or without reading their works. But rich traditions of ideas that originated in ancient Athens, that reached their high point in thinkers like Denis Diderot and particularly Hegel, and that still haunt us in the works of R. G. Collingwood and Hans Jonas, are ignored. (Need I add that social theory suffers even more, especially from a lack of in-depth study of Rousseau, Marx, and Kropotkin.) Nor is Western thought made artificially relevant to ecological thinking by turning Spinoza into a Buddhist—a kind of "woodpath" that was first cleared years ago, when Erich Fromm tried to turn

Marx into a Zen master. To orientalize—California style—thinkers whose work emerged from distinctly Western problematics and traditions not only violates Western traditions and their integrity but serves to obscure both the contributions and the failings of these thinkers, thereby distorting them.

What is especially important is that the Western organismic tradition is much sturdier in its thrust than the Eastern. All too often, what "eco"-faddists unknowingly take from the West is not its organismic tradition but, ironically, its static analytical positivistic logic, a way of reasoning that stands at odds with organismic tendencies—even as they turn to the East for poetry to satisfy their more spiritualistic proclivities. This oddly schizophrenic ideological mutation has produced a strange twist in philosophical thinking within today's ecology movement: even as its mind is Western in its harsh instrumental methodology, its heart is uncritically Eastern in its sentimentality. The strange combination of a Western "mind," in its most instrumental and analytical positivistic form, with an Eastern "heart," at its most vaporous and squamous, cannot be resolved by a gospel of peaceable coexistence but must ultimately yield a total contradiction. Ecology's "pop" culture is at war with its own logical underpinnings.

Today's eclecticism jumbles together thinkers whose ideas are, to say the least, unrelated. In the academy, an incoherent body of "ecophilosophy" has emerged—a catchall "receptacle" (to borrow a metaphor from Plato's *Timaeus*) that wildly mixes tendencies that are sharply at variance with each other logically but that coexist in a blissful state of ignorance emotionally. To roll together Heidegger's ineffable "openness to Being" and Barry Commoner's trite cafeteria "ecology," with its maxim that there is "no such thing as a free lunch" in nature, is adolescent at best and insidious at worst. It asks us to descend from the Bavarian Alps to a New Jersey shopping mall without even popping an eardrum.

Typical of this eclecticism is "deep ecology"—widely discussed at ecological conferences these days, even as participants contemplate what is "deeper" than "deep ecology." Yet its very name typifies a confusion in semantics. Leaving aside the problems of using the dimensional word *deep*, "shallow ecology"—intended as the technocratic counterpart of "deep ecology"—is hardly to be graced with the word *ecology* when it is in fact nothing more than *environmentalism*. Moreover, one can be very "deep" but profoundly wrong, as Cartesian philosophy and positivist theory reveal today. It does not help one's ecology—whether deep, shallow, or social—to fill in its gaps with some plaster borrowed from Taoism, mortar from Buddhism, concrete from Heidegger, and bricks from Spinoza, not to speak of mud from Commoner, Paul Ehrlich, and the like. Attempts to compost a great variety of views under a common rubric like "deep ecology" or "bioregionalism" are gravely misleading: there are differences within the ecology movement that are utterly at odds with each other, and their divergences are more important than their so-called "common goal."

There is, in fact, an organismic tradition in Western thought that is at least as rich as that of the East. Moreover, longstanding debates in the Western tradition have engaged philosophers with highly important problems that the East has not confronted as fully; indeed, the Western organismic tradition is much sturdier in its thrust than the Eastern. One does not have to travel far into Eastern thought to find dualisms that are no less intractable than Descartes's and notions of dominating nature that are no less strident than Bacon's. Issues of monism and dualism, reductionism and dialectic, and the sometimes adversarial relationships between them were articulated, exacerbated, and confronted more clearly in the West—particularly in the works of Aristotle, Spinoza, and Hegel—than in the East, where these notions tended to take a vaporous and mystical form.

If my approach seems too "Eurocentric," let me warn the reader that Asian "centricity" is a greater affliction. It is the issues that ecological thinking raises, rather than geopolitical and demographic considerations, that should guide us here. Ultimately, the real questions that confront us are not only how to *feel* ecologically but how to *think* ecologically. The chasm between thought and feeling is growing wider today, not narrowing, despite the deluge of orientalized Westernisms that have descended upon us methodologically and the Westernized orientalisms that have descended upon us ontologically. It would be well, for a moment, to work with one tradition on its own ground and see what problems it raises and what solutions it advances.

NATURE PHILOSOPHY—EAST AND WEST

To think ecologically is to enter the domain of nature philosophy. This can be a very perilous step. Serious political ambiguities persist in nature philosophy itself: namely, its potential to nourish reaction as well as revolution. Contemporary society is still seared by images of nature that have fostered highly reactionary political views. Vaporous slogans about "community" and humanity's "oneness with nature" easily interplay with the legacy of "naturalistic" nationalism that reached its genocidal apogee in Nazism, with its myths of race and "blood and soil." It requires only a minor ideological shift from the ideas of the nineteenth-century Romantic movement and William Blake's mystical anarchism to arrive at Richard Wagner's mystical nationalism.

Nor does science, for all its claims to objectivity, rescue us from the waywardness of a nature philosophy tinged with romanticism and mysticism. The "naturalistic" injunctions with which Hitler initiated his blood-drenched march through Europe have their counterpart in the cosmic "laws" of natural history with which Stalin ideologically justified his blood-drenched industrialization of Russia. "Dialectical materialism," or "diamat"—which Friedrich Engels restated as "laws" like the "unity of opposites," the transformation of "quantity into quality," and the "negation of the negation"—anchored social development in an almost mechanistic causality that was as damning to modern claims of individuality and freedom as it was to the complex relationships of society to nature.

It is worth noting that the major theorists of the Frankfurt School, whose ideas are so fashionable these days, foundered on the horns of dilemmas that nature philosophy poses. Theodor Adorno and Max Horkheimer's dark pessimism about the human condition stemmed in large part from their inability to anchor an emancipatory ethics in a radically conceived ecological philosophy. Indeed, reason, in their view, was hopelessly tainted by its origin (as they understood it) as a means for dominating nature—a vast, presumably civilizatory enterprise that also required the domination of human by human as mere instruments of production. Marxist theory justified human servitude and the development of classes as unavoidable steps in humanity's "tortured" march toward freedom from material want and hopefully from social domination itself.[2] Such ideas, which traditional Marxism and liberalism celebrated and over which the Frankfurt School brooded, were the received wisdom of the last century. Hence the inability of so many radical theorists today to grapple with nature philosophy, dialectic, or indeed, any organic approach that seeks to reinterpret these outlooks ecologically. The domain of nature as a ground for freedom has been rendered taboo by the political consequences of earlier interpretations, many of which have mystified, romanticized, or unified nature and its relationship to society by means of a cosmic mysticism that preempts reason by intuition.

On the other hand, the fact that Eastern sages thought and felt profoundly does not immunize their work to the criticism that ambiguity clouds much of it. The Tao Te Ching, imputed to Lao-tzu, can be read not only as the peasantry's "way" for moving with the "grain" of nature but as a handbook for elitist control of the peasantry—an ambiguity that is no less troubling than the fact that Plato's *Republic* can be read not only as a far-seeing disquisition on justice but as a Hellenic guide for a guardian elite in the manipulation of the people. Western acolytes of Eastern thought often use such ambiguity to their advantage, exploiting metaphors of Eastern sages to render completely self-contradictory arguments intelligible, if not exactly coherent. Ambiguity is no virtue in itself; rather, it demands clarification and elucidation.

When many quasi-religious Asian tracts are viewed from a *social* standpoint—which social ecology always requires—some of their ambiguity seems to disappear. In traditional China, a fatalistic peasantry was an easily manipulable peasantry, however "softly" it dealt with nature—which was not quite as "soft" as the Western imagination tends to picture it. In this respect, Leon E. Stover's *The Cultural Ecology of Chinese Civilization* is a much-needed companion reader to Taoist and Buddhist literature.[3] The peasant village or Green Circle *(ch'ing chuan)* of the north—a sobriquet that Stover applies to Chinese villages generally—was traditionally the object of systematic plunder by an elite. This elite fostered a privileged "high culture" that patently justified their exploitation of the peasantry in the name of a "Great Connected Whole." What was "great," alas, was often what lay in the best interests of those who considered themselves "great," not necessarily of the peasantry, who also formed part of the "whole." Ecologically, the language of "connectedness" in the Tao Te Ching is enchantingly "naturalistic." Socially, however, it provided a rhetorical patina for unchallenged despotism in which peasant and elite were "connected" not by a mutualistic symbiosis but by a parasitism in which the peasant was the host and the gentleman the parasite.

Folk culture was separated from high culture by the illiteracy and contraction of the peasant village to an introverted, parochial, and self-enclosed universe—one that kept Chinese society fragmented, hierarchical, and socially immobile. Villagers' conceptions of nature were disconcerting: human life was seen in the most passive and resigned perspective, as a steady demographic flow into the "Sink of Death." Even divested of its institutional and ideological trappings, Taoism historically almost certainly shaped the peasantry into a social body without choice, motivation, respite from poverty, or hope of escaping being drained into the "Sink." In a "naturalistic" credo less of nurture than of unrelenting destiny, piety was intermingled with acquiescence toward one's fate, and toil was intermingled with "sanctimonious husbandry," as Stover calls it. From the viewpoint of the elite, the peasants' pride in their husbandry was less important than their vulnerability to exploitation.[4]

It is not my purpose to dwell at any great length on the Asian heart that so often dazzles the Western head. What is more important here is that this head is more mechanistic, instrumental, and inorganic than it cares to admit. Much that passes for ecological thinking today is as dim methodologically as it is starry-eyed ideologically. Behind the "Third Wave" that is rolling over us, the "new paradigm" that is shifting us, the "feedback" that is electrifying us, and the "woodpaths" that are guiding us, is a bizarre form of thinking that is as airy on its spiritual peaks as it is crudely mechanistic at its hypothetico-deductive base. These contradictory "ecological zones," as it were, reflect serious ambiguities in nature philosophy itself: namely, its potential to nourish reaction as well as revolution, often with the same visions that fed a Blake at one extreme and a Wagner at the other. These "ecological zones" must be briefly surveyed if the project of thinking ecologically is to be seriously explored.

SPIRITUAL MECHANISM

At the peril of standing very much at odds with what is voiced these days in ecological philosophy, let me say that the problem of dualism—the mode of thought that counterposes mind to body, thought to reality, and society to nature—which receives so much emphasis in ecological literature is giving way to the more serious problem of reductionism.

Dualism and reductionism, in fact, are usually deeply entangled with each other. A crude dualism tends to foster its counterpart in an equally crude monism that simplifies all of reality into a single, often homogeneous agency, force, substance, or energy source. Hegel caustically called this "a night in which all cows are black." The mystical sparks of light that appear in this "night" should not deceive us. That reductionist notions glimmer with words like Spirit, cosmic energy, vital forces, and *energy centers* barely conceals the fact that reductionism emerges from ways of thinking that are no less mechanistic, instrumental, and analytical than the hypothetico-deductive mentality that has assumed such supremacy over the past two centuries of Western thought. Seemingly mystical, spiritual, and even organismic conclusions are often deduced by means of hypothetico-deductive approaches, which in turn infect the entire project of "reenchanting" the world with dismally "disenchanting" instrumental underpinnings. Indeed, as we shall see, "method" can never be blandly detached from the content it yields, just as the means one uses in politics and life generally significantly determines the ends one pursues.

One has only to consider the current love affair between ecological philosophy and systems theory to observe this reductionism in its most popular, untutored, and syncretic form. Fritjof Capra's widely read *The Turning Point* can be taken as an example. "The creative unfolding of life toward forms of ever increasing complexity," we learn, "remained an unsolved mystery for more than a century after Darwin, but recent study has outlined the contours of a theory of evolution that promises to shed light on this striking characteristic of living organisms. This is a systems theory that focuses on the dynamics of self-transcendence and is based on the work of a number of scientists from various disciplines"—he mentions, among others, Ilya Prigogine, Gregory Bateson, and Ervin Laszlo, to single out those who are widely known in the United States. Capra continues:

The basic dynamics of evolution, according to the new systems view, begins with a system of homeostasis—a state of dynamic balance characterized by multiple independent fluctuations. When the system is disturbed it has the tendency to maintain its stability by means of negative feedback mechanisms, which tend to reduce the deviation from the balanced state. However, this is not the only possibility. Deviations may also be reinforced internally through positive feedback, either in response to environmental changes or spontaneously without any external influence. The stability of a living system is continually tested by its fluctuations, and at certain moments one or several of them may become so strong that they drive the system over an instability into an entirely new structure, which will again be fluctuating and relatively stable. The stability of living systems is never absolute. It will persist as long as the fluctuations remain below a critical size, but any system is always ready to transform itself, always ready to evolve. This basic model for evolution, worked out for chemical dissipative structures by Prigogine and his collaborators, has since been applied successfully to describe the evolution of various biological, social, and ecological systems.[5]

Almost everything that is troubling about spiritual mechanism, from its terminology to its thought, is contained in this telling passage. Systems theory is certainly useful in explaining the operation of systems, especially ones so structured as to lend themselves to systems theory analysis, just as the equations of physics can explain any phenomenon that can be reduced to the terms of physics. What serious people in ecological philosophy have to ask themselves is whether evolution, let alone self-transcendence, can really be reduced to "dynamics," "interdependent fluctuations," "feedback mechanisms"—or even "inputs" and "outputs"—that do not differ in principle from the Newtonian orientation toward phenomena or from La Mettrie's eighteenth-century description of human beings as machines. If there is anything developmental or evolutionary (as distinguished from merely kinetic) about a systems theory "paradigm," it is simply that some relatively homeostatic phenomena, conceived precisely as systems, may be replaced with other, hopefully complex systems. In either case, despite the imagery that Capra tries to form in the reader's mind, we cannot properly speak of one mechanism being qualitatively transformed into another. If the essential problem of organic development is reduced at all its levels to "feedback loops" and "fluctuations," our thinking has not advanced beyond Cartesian and Hobbesian mechanism, however lavishly we speak of the "coevolution of an organism *plus* its environment," of "wholeness," or of Taoist sagacity and Franciscan theology.[6]

There is a physical basis to everything that physics— "Taoist," Newtonian, or Prigoginian—describes with varying degrees of exactness and at various levels of physical development. But this fact is no more a warrant for casting *all* phenomena in terms of these descriptions than reducing the entire world to matter and motion. Indeed, such reductionism is fatal to any form of organismic thinking. Capra's explication of a systems theory of evolution describes thought as "free."[7] But to speak of "autonomy and freedom of choice" in nature, pure and simple, is to diminish the ethical meaning of the words. Nature may be an evolving *ground* for autonomy, freedom, and an increasing measure of choice, but a ground *is no more identical with the ethics it sustains* than nutrients in soil are identical with the plants they sustain. Autonomy and freedom presuppose human intellection, the power to conceptualize and generalize. Their domain must be explicated in cultural, logical, and, within very definite limits, biological terms—not in terms of a cosmic "dynamics" that is "basically open and indeterminate."[8] Indeed, to flippantly confuse indeterminacy with autonomy and openness with freedom is to shift from one level to another as carelessly as one stirs a cup of tea. Capra's approach to "freedom" renders indeterminacy and statistical probability in physics coequal with human social freedom, without the least regard for the staggering complexity of social institutions, wayward individual proclivities, diverse cultural traditions, and conflicting personal wills.

Ilya Prigogine has attempted to explain the organic process of evolution through "chemical dissipative structures," in which various systems are formed in succession, each hopefully of greater complexity than the ones that preceded it.[9] In a succession of systems, these "dissipative structures," which can be mathematically formulated, are shown to succeed each other: a system approaches a "far from equilibrium" situation, which marks its transition to a new system. Here, as "dissipative structures" replace the phases of growth, development gives way to thermodynamics. Nor does a system of positive feedback, upon which Prigoginian systems theory depends, *allow for a concept of potentiality:* it is rather *chance and stochastic phenomena* that act as "mediating" phases between one "dissipative structure" and another. Confronted with "far from equilibrium" disorder and succeeding orderly systems, speculative thought is reduced to mere observation. Indeed, a system approaching transition may not assume an immanently predictable form thereafter—it may simply fall apart into "chaos." These systems have, in effect, no internal developmental logic.

Prigogine's mathematics can no more explain the biological, social, and personal differentiae that make up reality, even with the aid of winged Taoist metaphors, than a heap of bricks can form itself into a Gothic cathedral through the "fluctuations" involved in positive feedback. One could, with equal aplomb, try to reduce organic metabolism to Einstein's cosmic formula $E = mc^2$, simply because it is cosmic. At the risk of adding to philosophy's already heavy burden of "fallacies," I would define the "reductionist fallacy" as the application of the most general formulas to the most detailed particulars, in the belief that what is universal and seemingly all-encompassing must necessarily explain what is highly particular and uniquely individual.[10] At best, a formula, a "paradigm," or more properly, a philosophy, may provide the basis for an orientation toward reality at a clearly definable level of reality. Ironically, the more universal, abstract, and mathematical a formula is, the more likely that its very generality will limit it when it is applied to concrete, highly particularized phenomena. $E = mc^2$ is *too* cosmic to explain such richly articulated or mediated modes of reality as natural evolution, organic metabolism, social development, and personal behavior.

Not surprisingly, New Age acolytes of ecology become authentic reductionists. "God," "Energy," "Being," "Love," "Interconnectedness," and a whole repertoire of metaphors are invoked that serve to homogenize the particular and divest it of its richness and diversity. When this approach proves too abstract, it is always possible to create a pastiche of ill-digested "paradigms" and theories, regardless of the fact that their premises and logic may conflict with each other. Here eclecticism, which usually clouds radically different ways of thinking and the myth that we all share a "common goal," becomes the last redoubt for sheer intellectual sloppiness.

The language that the more sophisticated systems theorists use reflects the concepts they bring to their "paradigms." Complex results are stripped down to their most elemental levels so that they can be handled in physico-mathematical terms. That hypothetico-deductive analyses have immense value in relations that are authentically dynamic or mechanical is not in question here; their value in these domains of knowledge cannot be surpassed. What is troubling is that systems theory tends to become a highly imperialistic ideological approach that stakes out a claim to the totality of development, indeed to reason out and explain virtually all phenomena. *If* natural evolution, organic metabolism, and personal behavior were systems, *then* systems theory in all its self-fulfilling grandeur would seem to work admirably. That this "if-then" conversion (and I will have more to say about these later) denudes phenomena of many complex qualities that do not lend themselves to systems analysis is conveniently lost in a shuffle of grandiose metaphors that appeal more to an ever-yielding heart than to a demanding logical mind.

By contrast, the power of the West's organismic—more precisely, dialectical—tradition (even at Hegel's highly conceptual level) lies in *building up* the differentiae of natural and social phenomena from what is implicit in their abstract level—not in corrosively *reducing* their richly articulated concreteness to abstract, logically manipulable "data." The difference between the two approaches could not be stated sharply enough. Dialectic, as we shall see, tries to elicit the development of phenomena from their level of abstract "homogeneity," latent with the rich differentiation that will mark their maturity, while systems theory tries to *reduce* phenomena from their highly articulated particularity to the level of homogeneous abstraction so necessary for mathematical symbolization. Dialectic, in effect, is a logic of evolution *from abstraction toward differentiation;* systems theory is a logic of devolution *from differentiation toward abstraction.*

For the present, it is important to note that the careless use of the word *complexity* often tells us nothing whatever about the nature of a complex phenomenon and its development, anymore than the careless use of the word *process* tells us anything about the nature of a complex process. Many complex phenomena, viewed in an ethical or even in a survival sense, are positively harmful and woefully unecological, such as the complex, presumably self-regulating market—whose advocates are, in fact, captivated by the theoretical premises of Prigogine's version of systems theory. Nor can we ignore complex processes that can degrade a biologically desirable development, such as epidemics that exterminate ecologically valuable species.

Development without a "goal in it, or purpose," as Capra declares somewhat dolefully, can be equally meaningless, despite the fact that his "systems theory of life" finds a "recognizable pattern of development."[11] The word *pattern*—or for that matter, *paradigm*—is no substitute for the idea of *tendency* in speculative philosophy. In the absence of everything but a system of positive feedback that may or may not yield complexity, Capra, like many of his associates, is obliged to turn to the East and import an ethics to render systems theory meaningful—even in flat contravention of his Western methodology. In a sudden leap, the language (not to speak of the conceptual framework) of *The Turning Point* undergoes a startling transformation. Invocations of "a new holistic worldview," "a conceptual shift from structure to rhythm"—extended to the "rise and fall" of civilizations, indeed to the "planet as a whole ... as it spins around its axis and moves around the sun"—suddenly overlie the "dynamics" and "feedback loops" that actually form the eminently Western methodological underpinnings of his "systems view of life." "Eastern mystical traditions, especially in Taoism," are thrown into a potpourri of formulations whose only similarity is metaphoric.[12] "The idea of fluctuations as the basis of order is one of the basic themes in Taoist texts," Capra apprises us, making it seem in the most superficial way that Taoism parallels Prigogine's systems approach. But "fluctuations," like "cycles," have been used from time immemorial to explain stagnation rather than evolution, fixity rather than change, and eternality rather than development. Syncretically placing fluctuations in systems theory on a par with fluctuations in Taoism is about as sound as placing the electromagnetic "attraction" in physics on par with Eros as a "cosmic" source of affinity and unity. From a methodological viewpoint, Prigogine's mathematical formulation of chemical dissipative structures fits just as snugly into Newton's mechanistic sensibility as the corpuscular theory of light fits into the wave theory. These conceptual frameworks meld together because they derive from the same hypothetico-deductive, indeed clearly mechanistic mentality.

Nor is it helpful to recast the "systems view of life" into Gregory Bateson's theoretical framework. Here, materiality is dissolved into interrelationships and then subjectivized as "minds." This framework might be somewhat comprehensible to an Eastern sage, but it divests substance, indeed nature itself, of its very physicality. Abandoning the study of things—living or not—for a study of the relationships between them is as one-sided and reductionist as abandoning the study of relationships for the things they interrelate. If traditional materialist mechanism strongly emphasized the object, often with results that inhibited speculation beyond the given state of affairs, Bateson's emphasis on relationships verges on a subjectivism that could almost be taken for solipsism if one did not know more about Bateson's work as a whole. The claim that "all experience is subjective" and that "our brains make the images that we think we 'perceive'" borders on an idealist counterpart of Jacob Moleschott's equally crude materialist maxim, "No thought without phosphorus."[13]

Thinking once presupposed a knowledge of thought as it unfolded over millennia of philosophical and social development. Today, the intellectual span of the present generation barely extends beyond a decade and is marked by a disquieting bias in favor of journalistic glibness. That ecological acolytes of systems theory often merely stand Newtonian mechanism on its head yet receive no criticism from ecologically oriented intellectuals is evidence of the cultural Dark Ages that are gathering around us. We are even witnessing a revival of Hume's "is-ought" criticism, which denies speculative thought the right to reason from the "what-is" to the "what-should-be." This positivistic mousetrap is a problem not in logic but in ethics—notably, the right of the ethical "should-be" to enjoy an objective status. The problem of constituting an objective ethics, which confounded the Frankfurt School, is no less serious than Hume's quarrel with organized religion. Speculative philosophy by definition claims that reason can project *beyond* the given state of affairs, whether to Plato's exemplary domain of forms or Marx and Kropotkin's visions of a cooperative society. To remain within the "what-is" in the name of logical consistency is to deny reason the right to assert goals, values, and social relationships that provide a voice to the claims of ecology as a social discipline.

These theoretical problems have an eminently practical significance. In all cases they reveal an intellectual glibness that dissolves that which is concrete in the ecological picture, indeed the life-forms that give substantially to the various systems, into interrelationships, "dynamics," and "minds" that Capra, Prigogine, Bateson, et al., abstract into lifeless categories. Thus reductionism not only turns complex organisms and their equally complex evolution into mechanical "fluctuations," debasing concrete organisms into abstract interrelationships; it turns life in all its rich specificity into an abstraction, thereby divesting nature of the variety, indeed the species-individuality so essential to an understanding of nature's fecundity and its evolutionary impetus.[14]

HUMANISM AND ANTIHUMANISM

"Humanity," currently so unfulfilled and divided against itself, has scarcely realized its potentialities. But in much current "ecological" thinking the concept of humanity is no less sucked into the ideological black hole.[15] Ideologically, the phenomenon of human self-hatred (and human beings seem to be the one species that has the ability to luxuriate in self-hatred) takes a number of forms: a logically ambiguous "biocentrism" and often strident antihumanism are set against "anthropocentrism" and humanism—presumably the cardinal sins of an abstract "Man," who is determined to despoil an equally abstract "Nature." If systems theory divests nonhuman life of its specificity, biocentrism and antihumanism divest human life of social development. Society becomes an abstraction that somehow is inflicted upon "Nature" without any regard for such social characteristics as hierarchy, domination, and the state. As a result, a simplistic biologism emerges, often structured around "natural laws," that sees "Man" and humanism as a curse that afflicts "Nature" with ecological degradation. As a result, some voices in the ecology movement call for a moral "biospheric democracy" in which humanity's "right" to live and fulfill itself is equatable with that same "right" in butterflies, ants, whales, apes, and—yes—pathogenic viruses and germs.

Viewed heuristically, biocentrism is an effort to bridle "human" arrogance toward other life-forms and defy the present destruction of the biosphere. But how long one can continue to belabor "humanity" for its affronts to the biosphere without distinguishing between rich and poor, men and women, whites and people of color, exploiters and exploited, is a nagging problem that many ecological philosophers have yet to resolve, or perhaps even recognize. Biocentrism, for all the caveats its supporters issue to qualify it, strikes me as bluntly misanthropic and less an ecological principle than an argument against the human species itself as a life-form.

Taken separately, perhaps, the intentions of their adherents may be good, even as these theories are seriously faulty. United into a single ensemble, however, they develop a harsh logic and create an arena for explicitly vicious views. It was not surprising that David Foreman, then of Earth First! and an avowed acolyte of "deep ecology," could advance the following "ecological" verdict on the Third World:

> When I tell people how the worst thing we could do in Ethiopia is to give aid—the best thing would be to just let nature seek its own balance, to let the people there just starve ... they think that is monstrous. But the alternative is that you go in and save these half-dead children who never will live a whole life. Their development will be stunted. And what's going to happen in ten years' time is that twice as many people will suffer and die.
>
> Likewise, letting the USA be an overflow valve for problems in Latin America is not solving a thing. It's just putting more pressure on resources we have in the USA. It is just causing more destruction of our wilderness, more poisoning of water and air, and it isn't helping the problems in Latin America.[16]

Regrettably, it is all too easy to interpret such remarks as an apologia for imperialism, racism, and genocide. To consider starvation as merely an "alternative" to the civil war that wracked Ethiopia and the destruction of so much of the cultural integrity of Latin American villages by (largely American) corporate interests reveals a shocking social amnesia. It is breathtaking to contemplate the extent to which this "ecological" ensemble of ideas deflects public attention from the *social origins* of ecological problems. That anything besides "nature" is seeking its "balance" in the Third World seems to elude Foreman, whose obfuscation of social problems expresses the logic of a reductionist "ecology." Such "reverence for the earth" stifles even the modest decencies of middle-class virtues like empathy and concern for the plight of hungry children. "Earth wisdom" of this kind could well leave us with a "love" of the planet but no care for the underprivileged who make up so much of the human species.

Yet Foreman's remarks are not idiosyncratic. Quite to the contrary: an authoritarian streak is latent in a crude biologism that conceals an ever-diminishing humaneness with "natural law" and papers over the fact that it is *capitalism* that is at work here, not an abstract "Humanity" and "Society." This authoritarian mentality sometimes coexists with pious appeals to variants of Eastern spirituality, placing a saintly mask on the ruthless egoism that stems from bourgeois greed. "Ecological thinking" of this kind is all the more sinister because it subverts the organic, indeed dialectical thinking that can rescue us from reductionism. An unbridgeable gulf separates social ecology from the neo-Malthusianism that the ensemble of biocentrism, anti-humanism, and "natural law" theory have spawned. We are grimly in need of a "reenchantment" of humanity—to use the quasi-mystical jargon of our day—with a fluid, organismic, and dialectical rationality. For it is in this *human* rationality that nature ultimately actualizes its own evolution of subjectivity over long aeons of neural and sensory development. *There is nothing more natural than humanity's capacity to conceptualize, generalize, relate ideas, engage in symbolic communication, and innovate changes in the world around it, not merely to adapt to the conditions it finds at hand.* For biocentric, antihumanist, and "natural law" advocates to set their faces against the self-realization of nature in an ecologically oriented humanity and dialectical thought is to foster the image of a blighted humanity. No less than Adam and Eve's acquisition of knowledge, humanity's power of thought becomes its abiding "original sin."

ECOLOGIZING THE DIALECTIC

It is eminently *natural* for humanity to create a "second nature" from its evolution in "first nature." By *second nature,* I mean the development of uniquely human culture, with a wide variety of institutionalized human communities, effective human technics, richly symbolic languages, and carefully managed sources of nutriment. Dualism, in all its forms, has opposed these two natures to each other, as antagonists. Monism, in turn, often dissolves one into the other—be it liberalism, fascism, or more recently, the biocentrism that so closely approximates misanthropic antihumanism. These monist ideologies differ primarily in whether they want to dissolve first nature into second or second nature into first.

What these dualisms and monisms have in common is an acceptance of domination. Classically, the counterpart of the "domination of nature by man" has been the "domination of man by nature." Just as Marxism and liberalism see the former as a desideratum that emerges out of the latter, so enthusiasts of "natural law" accept the latter as a fact and condemn efforts to achieve the former. These views are deeply flawed—not only because they are conceptually one-sided or simply wrong, but because of the way they are philosophically structured and worked out. The real question, I submit, is not whether second nature parallels, opposes, or blandly "participates" in an "egalitarian" first nature;[17] rather, it is how second nature is *derived* from first nature. More specifically, in what ways did the highly graded and many-phased evolution from first nature into second give rise to social institutions, forms of interactions between people, and an interaction between first and second nature that, in the best of cases, enriches both and yields a second nature that has an evolutionary development of its own? The ecological crisis we face today is very much a crisis in the emergence of society out of biology, in the problems (the rise of hierarchy, domination, patriarchy, classes, and the state) that unfolded with this development, and in the liberatory pathways that provide an alternative to this warped history.

The fact that first and second nature exist and can never be dualized into "parallels" or simplistically reduced to each other accounts, in great part, for my phrase *social ecology*. Additionally, social ecology has the special meaning that the ecological crisis that beleaguers us stems from a social crisis, a crisis that the crude biologism of "deep ecology" generally ignores. Still further, that the resolution of this social crisis can only be achieved by reorganizing society along rational lines, imbued with an ecological philosophy and sensibility.

Such a philosophy and sensibility cannot be eclectically patched together from bits and pieces of mechanism and mysticism, or of conventional reason and Eastern spirituality. One could respect a consistently Eastern mystical view or a consistently Western mechanistic view, however one-sided or erroneous each may be. But neither view can fruitfully derive second nature from first nature organically. That requires a mode of thought that distinguishes the phases of the evolutionary continuum from which second nature emerges and yet preserves first nature as part of the process. Common sense betrays us with its demand for conceptual fixity; mysticism, in turn, deflects us from rationality that goes substantially beyond poetic metaphors. A good deal of ecological thinking today, as we have seen, partakes of both modes—the mechanistic and the mystical—in an opportunistic, "catch-as-catch-can" manner, rather than restructuring its mode of thought in an authentically organic manner.

This much should be clear: the purely deductive logic that we use to build bridges, budget our income and expenses, plan our everyday lives, and calculate our chances of "making out" in the world holds no promise of grasping the richly articulated or mediated development that both unites and differentiates first and second nature. Common sense demands only inference, consistency, and the verification that ordinary sensory experience provides. Apart from the inductively apprehended particulars that help us arrive (often quite intuitively) at the concrete premises for our inferences, we normally tend to deduce our ideas schematically, as a series of well-ordered and rigidly fixed concepts. Truth in this everyday logical domain is normally little more than consistency. Thus, we are held to be "logical" when our conclusions can be framed into fixed categories—supported, to be sure, by those atomized isolates known as "brute facts." This achievement is celebrated as "clarity" and its results as "certainty." To conceive of any form of reasoning other than a hypothetico-deductive logic is evidence of fuzzy-headedness. Facts, you know, are facts, and truth is truth. Consistency, the formalistic "if-then" propositions that make up conventional logic, together with experience as a sequence of "clear-cut" data and the eminently practical results that conventional logic achieves—all, taken together, are the means to "think clearly" and understand the "real world."

Yet there is a highly personal sphere of life in which we think very differently from conventional reason. We do not deal with children the way we deal with our business affairs and the pragmatics of everyday living. We see children as *developing* beings who pass through necessary phases of growth and increasing capabilities. We try not to impose more demands upon them than they can adequately handle at their age (assuming, to be sure, that we are rational and humane people). Nor do we try to afflict them with problems they cannot yet resolve. We sense a flow in their lives that involves the actualization of their potentialities at different levels of their development. It requires no unusual perception to recognize the infant that lingers on in the child, the child that lingers on in the youth, the youth that lingers on in the adult—in short, the *cumulative* nature of human development, in contrast to mere substitution and succession. Only a fool believes that the man or woman could—or should—completely replace the boy or girl. Properly understood, a mature person is not an inventory of test results and measurements. He or she is an individual *biography,* the developmental embodiment of partially or wholly realized qualities that an environment surely conditions but whose inherent makeup would ultimately determine his or her development *if* society acquired a highly rational form.

However intuitive it may be, this kind of thinking is structured around not deduction but *eduction.* If deduction consists of the inferential "if-then" steps we take, with due reverence for consistency, to arrive at unshakable and clearly defined judgments about "brute facts," eduction fully manifests and articulates the latent possibilities of phenomena. Eduction is a phased process in which "if" is not a fixed hypothetical premise but rather a *potentiality.* "Steps" in eduction are not mere inferences but stages of *development.* "Consistency," far from being an imposed canon of logic based on principles of identity, contradiction, and the excluded middle, is the immanent process we properly call *self-development.* Finally, "then" is the full *actualization* of potentiality in its rich, self-incorporative "stages" of growth, differentiation, maturation, and wholeness. That the "mature" and "whole" are never so complete that they cease to be the potentiality for a still further development represents an ecological change I am advancing here.

Which brings us to the problem of what we are obliged to modify in the dialectical philosophy of its two most outstanding voices, Aristotle and Hegel, in order to render it an *ecological* mode of thought.[18] To do this, we must briefly summarize what an ecological dialectic shares with the Aristotelian and Hegelian. Dialectical philosophy moves from the undifferentiated abstract to the highly differentiated concrete (while most commonsensical forms of thought move in the opposite direction). In this respect dialectic picks up the thread of classical eduction and goes beyond it, moving from that which is implicit in bare potentiality to its realization in a fully articulated actuality. Much of Greek philosophy expressed this problematic as that of the emergence of the Many from the One: in Aristotle's work, the apogee of classical thought, "a conception of substance, or the real, as the goal toward which develops a potential being that, save as ultimately realized, is neither real nor intelligible, dominates the whole course of Aristotle's speculation," observes G.R.G. Mure in a very pithy formulation. "Follow him as he applies it in every sphere which he investigates; watch it grow from this initial abstract formula into a concrete universe of thought; and you may hope to grasp the essential meaning of his philosophy."[19] The same could be said of Hegel, whose elaboration of this Aristotelian motif is more subjectivized and informed, although at times it is cluttered by the mountain of problematics that had been added to Western philosophy since Aristotle's time.

An ecological dialectic would have to address the fact that Aristotle and Hegel did not work with an evolutionary theory of nature but rather saw the natural world more as a scala naturae, a ladder of "Being," than as a flowing continuum. An ecological dialectic introduces evolution into this tradition and replaces the notion of a scala naturae with a richly mediated continuum. Both thinkers were more profoundly influenced by Plato than their writings would seem to indicate, with the result that in the case of Hegel, we move within a realm of concepts more than history (however historical Hegel's dialectic invariably was). Hegel was strongly preoccupied with the "idea" of nature rather than with its existential details, although he honored this preoccupation in the breach. Finally, the overarching teleology of the two philosophers tends to subordinate the contingency, spontaneity, and creativity that mark natural phenomena.[20] Hegel, with his strong theological bent, terminated the unfolding of the world in an "Absolute" that encompasses it in an identity of subject and object. In an ecological dialectic, by contrast, there would be no terminality that could culminate in a God or an Absolute. "Actuality," to use Hegel's special term, is the almost momentary culmination of maturity, so that the objectivity of the potential, which is crucial for an objective ethics, is subordinated to its actualization.

English translations of Hegel often erroneously render *real* and *actual* as synonyms in certain passages, allowing the

Hegelian "real" to be conceived as the actualization of the potential —a failing that I believe should be corrected. What is less "real" than Hegel's "reality"—notably the "brute facts" or the given "is" of common sense—would more closely correspond to what Hegel considers "the apparent" (*das Erscheinende*). From an ecological viewpoint, this mistranslation could lead to much confusion. Hence, I have used the word *real* to mean simply "what-is," not "what is necessarily latent in the potential." The *actual* remains very much what Hegel meant it to mean: the rational realization of the potential, as distinguished from the "real" as the existential.[21] Finally, an ecological dialectic greatly modifies the creative role that Hegel imparted to strife, often interpreted as mere "antithesis" (which is roughly as far as Theodor Adorno takes the dialectic in his *Negative Dialectics*), but not without ignoring the presence of strife in human history. It emphasizes that the dialectic, no less in Hegel's than in my own thinking, undergoes differentiation through a transcendence beyond mere antithesis, notably what Hegel called an *Aufhebung* or negation of the negation. Dialectic is thus a philosophy of progress in which there is a growing elaboration and self-consciousness, insofar as the world is rational.

Dialectic, let me emphasize, is not merely "change," "motion," or even "process," all banal imputations to the contrary notwithstanding. Nor can it be subsumed under "process philosophy." Dialectic is *development*, not only change; it is *derivation*, not only motion; it is *mediation*, not only process; and it is *cumulative*, not only continuous. That it is also change, motion, process, and a continuum tells us only part of its true content. But denied its immanent self-directiveness and its entelechial eduction of the potential into the actual, this "process philosophy," indeed this remarkable notion of *causality*, ceases to be dialectic. Instead, it becomes a mere husk that our current flock of "eco"-faddists can reduce to "kinetics," "dynamics," "fluctuations," and "feedback loops"—the same mechanistic verbiage with which systems theory dresses itself up as a developmental philosophy.

As Hegel warned in the course of educing the complexity of the dialectical process: knowledge has "no other object than to draw out what is inward or implicit and thus to become objective." But if

> that which is implicit comes into existence, it certainly passes into change, yet it *remains one and the same*. ... The plant, for example, does not lose itself in mere indefinite change. From the germ much is produced when at first nothing was to be seen; but the whole of what is brought forth, if not developed, is yet hidden and ideally contained within itself. The principle of *this projection into existence* is that the germ cannot remain merely implicit, but is impelled toward development, since it presents the contradiction of being only implicitly and yet not desiring to be so.[22]

Thus dialectic is not *wayward* motion, the mere kinetics of change. There is a rational "end in view"—not one that is preordained, to state this point from an ecological viewpoint rather than a theological one, but that actualizes what is implicit in the potential. Every "if-then" proposition is premised not on any *if* that springs into one's head like a gambler's hunch; it posits a potentiality that has its ancestry in the dialectical processes that preceded it.

Reductionism breaks this process down to the most undifferentiated interactions it can formulate. But it does so at the cost of demolishing the various phases or "moments" (to use Hegelian terminology) from which the process is literally constituted. A human being is clearly an ensemble of chemicals. While reductionism can explain its existence as a physico-chemical phenomenon, it cannot comprehend it as a remarkably complex form of life. Chemical analysis provides us with no substitute for the multitude of forms, relationships, processes, and environments that the organic creates for itself as it metabolically sustains its own "selfhood" in distinction from other "selves." Indeed, carried too far into a lower level of phenomena, reduction leads to dissolution, so that the very integrity of a given level of phenomena—be it social, biological, chemical, or physical—simply disappears into mere "matter" and "motion." In a kind of ideological entropy, thought no longer has the differentiae with which to define its subject matter, let alone explore it. As the complex is trimmed down to its "irreducible" components, the whole that forms the very premises of thought disappears into a meaningless, indeed formless heap of "matter," thereby erasing the very boundaries that give *definition* to a phenomenon as a component of a more complex "whole."

In the organic world, the metabolic activity of the simplest life-forms constitutes the sense of self-identity, however germinal, from which nature acquires a rudimentary subjectivity. Not only does this rudimentary subjectivity (which reductionism necessarily cannot encompass) derive from the metabolic process of self-maintenance, a process that defines any life-form as a unique whole; it extends itself beyond self-maintenance to become a *striving* activity, not unlike the development from the vegetative to the animative, that ultimately yields mind, will, and the potentiality for freedom. Conceived dialectically, organic evolution is, in a broad sense, subjective insofar as life-forms begin to exercise choices in adapting to new environments—a conception that stands much at odds with that clearly definable fixity we blissfully call "clear thinking." Systems theory enters into the reductionist tableau in a sinister way: by dissolving the subjective element in biological phenomena so that they can be treated as mathematical symbols, systems theory permits evolutionary interaction, subjective development, and even process itself, to be taken over by "the system," just as the individual, the family, and the community are destructured into "the System" embodied by the economic corporation and the state. Life ceases to have subjectivity and becomes a mechanism in which the tendency of life-forms toward ever-greater elaboration is replaced with "feedback loops," and their evolutionary antecedents with programmed "information." A "systems view of life" literally conceives of life as a system, not only as "fluctuations" and "cycles"—mechanistic as these concepts are in themselves.

Despite the external selective factors with which Darwinians describe evolution, the tendency of life toward a greater complexity of selfhood—a tendency that yields increasing degrees of subjectivity—constitutes the internal or immanent impulse of evolution toward growing self-awareness. This evolutionary dialectic constitutes the essence of life as a self-maintaining organism that bears the *potential* for the development of self-conscious organisms. Dialectic, in effect, is not merely a "logic" or a "method" that can be bounced around and "applied" promiscuously to a content. It has no "handbook" other than *reason itself* to guide those who seek to develop a dialectical sensibility. Dialectic can no more be applied to problems in engineering than Einstein's general theory of relativity can be applied to plumbing; these problems can best be resolved by conventional forms of logic, common sense, and the pragmatic knowledge acquired through experience. Dialectic can only explicate a rationally developmental phenomenon, just as systems theory can only explicate the workings of a fluctuating and cyclical system. The kind of verification that validates or invalidates the soundness of dialectical reasoning, in turn, must be *developmental*, not relatively static or for that matter "fluctuating" kinds of phenomena.

Hence, it distorts the very meaning of dialectic to speak of it as a "method." Indeed, dialectical philosophy, properly conceived and freed of mechanistic presumptions, is an ongoing protest against the myth of methodology: notably, that the "techniques" for thinking out a process can be separated from the process itself. Its sensitivity for concrete phenomena, even when they are distilled into "concepts," as Hegel did, is what renders dialectic such an existentially vital and palpably organismic philosophy. It was Hegel's genius to reintroduce Plato's supramundane world of forms—an *exemplary* and hence a *moral* world, not merely a metaphysical one—into reality and to develop Aristotle's notion of entelechy into a concept of "transcendence" (*Aufhebung*) that nuances processes as mediated "moments in the self-fulfillment of their potentialities." Freed of its theological trappings, dialectic *explains*, with a power beyond that of any conventional logic, how the organic flow of first into second nature is a reworking of biological into social reality. Each phase or "moment," pressed by its own internal logic into an antithetical and ultimately a more transcendent form, emerges as a more complex unity-in-diversity that encompasses its earlier moments even as it goes beyond them. Despite the imagery of strife that permeates the Hegelian version of this process, the ultimate point in the Hegelian *Aufhebung* is reconciliation, not the nihilism of pure negation. Moreover, norms—the actualization of the potential "is" into the ethical "ought"—are anchored in the objective reality of potentiality itself, not as it always "is," to be sure, but as it "should be," such that speculation becomes a valid account of reality in its truth. Hegel, I would argue, *radically expanded the very concept of Being in philosophy and in the real world to encompass the potential and its actualization into the rational "what-should-be,"* not only as an existential "what-is."[23]

Dialectical speculation, despite Hegel's own view of the retrospective function of philosophy, thus is *projective* in a sharply critical sense (quite unlike "futurology," which dissolves the future by making it a mere extrapolation of the present). In its restless critique of reality we can call dialectic a "negative philosophy"—in contrast, I should add, to Adorno's nihilism or "negative dialectics." By the same token, speculation is creative in that it ceaselessly contrasts the free, rational, and moral actuality of "what-could-be," which inheres in nature's thrust toward self-reflexivity, with the existential reality of "what-is."[24] Speculation can ask "why" (not only "how") the real has become the irrational—indeed, the inhuman and anti-ecological—precisely because dialectic alone is capable of grounding an ecological ethics in the potential, that is, in its objective possibilities for the realization of reason and truth.

This objectivization of possibilities—of potentiality continuous with its yet unrealized actualization—is the ground for a genuinely objective ethics, as distinguished from an ethical relativism subject to the waywardness of the opinion poll. An ecological dialectic, in effect, opens the way to an ethics that is rooted in the objectivity of the potential, not in the commandments of a deity or in the eternality of a supramundane and transcendental "reality." Hence, the "what-should-be" is not only objective, it forms the objective critique of the given reality.

Human intervention into nature is inherent and inevitable. To argue that this intervention should not occur is utterly obfuscatory, since humanity's second nature is not simply an external imposition on biology's first nature but is the result of first nature's inherent evolutionary process. What is at issue in humanity's transformation of nature is whether its practice is consistent with an objective ecological ethics that is rationally developed, not haphazardly divined, felt, or intuited. Minimally, such an ecological ethics would involve human stewardship of the planet. A humanity that failed to see that it is potentially nature rendered self-conscious and self-reflexive would separate itself from nature morally as well as intellectually. Second nature in such a situation would literally be divested of its last ties to first nature; worse, the vacuum left by the departure of consciousness would be filled by blind market-oriented interests and an egoistic marketplace mentality. In any case, there is no road back from second to first nature, any more than second nature as it is now constituted can rescue the biosphere from destruction with "technological fixes" and political reforms.

Given the massive ecological crisis that confronts us, intellectual confusion in the ecology movement may yield harmful results of immeasurable proportions. In the present period of history, to carelessly heap fragments of ideas upon each other and call this ecophilosophy is no longer an affordable luxury. Stewardship of the earth need not consist of such accommodating measures as the establishment of ecological wilderness zones or half measures to patch up environmental dislocations. What it can and should mean is a radical integration of second nature with first nature along far-reaching ecological lines, an integration that would yield new ecocommunities, ecotechnologies, and an abiding ecological sensibility that embodies nature's thrust toward self-reflexivity. For biocentrists and antihumanists to throw the word *arrogance* around whenever anyone cites human beings as ethical and mental referents for nature and natural evolution is manipulative. Nature without an active human presence would be as unnatural as a tropical rainforest that lacked monkeys and ants. Dialectic, it should be noted, is no less a critique of onesidedness and simplicity than of existing reality and an adaptive mentality to the status quo. Cast in radical ecological terms, it calls for a denial of *centricity* as such, be it "anthropocentricity," "biocentricity," or so-called "ecocentricity," which is meant to include rocks and rivers as well as life-forms. A philosophy of organic development is above all a philosophy of *wholeness* in which evolution reaches a degree of unity-in-diversity such that nature can *act* upon itself rationally through rational human agency, with its derivation in nature's potential for freedom and conceptual thought.

In the intermediate zone between first and second nature that saw the graded passage of biological evolution into social, social evolution began to assume increasingly hierarchical forms. Whether this could have been avoided is impossible to say—and meaningless to divine. In any case, social evolution unfolded in the direction of hierarchical, class-oriented, and statist institutions, giving rise to the nation-state and ultimately, albeit not inevitably, to a capitalist economy. In our own time, the massive penetration of this economy into society as a whole has produced an even more serious distortion of second nature. The market *economy*, which all cultures from antiquity to recent times have resisted to one degree or another, has essentially become a market *society*. This society is historically unique. It identifies progress with competition rather than cooperation. It views society as a realm for possessing things rather than for elaborating human relationships. It creates a morality based on growth rather than limit and balance. For the first time in human history, society and community have been reduced to little more than a huge shopping mall.

Unless ecology explores this warped development systematically—that is, unless it unearths its internal logic in a reasoned and organismic way—its critical thrust will be entirely lost and its integrity hopelessly impugned. Today, eclecticism and reductionism—a hodgepodge of disconnected, even contradictory ideas degraded to their lowest common denominator—are the most serious obstacles to the realization of this critical project. Eclecticism may appeal to lazy minds that prefer slogans to reasoned studies of society and its impact on the natural world. But with lazy minds come lazy thoughts and a passive-receptive mentality that increasingly renders the mind vulnerable to authoritarian control.

BEYOND FIRST AND SECOND NATURE

We must try to bring the threads of our discussion together and examine the important implications dialectic has for ecological thinking. A "dialectical view of life" is a special form of process philosophy. Its emphasis is not on change alone but on development. It is eductive rather than merely deductive, mediated rather than merely processual, and cumulative rather than merely continuous. Its objectivity begins with the existence of the potential, not with the mere facticity of the real; hence its ethics seeks the "what-should-be" as a realm of *objective* possibilities. That "possibilities" are objective, albeit not in the sense of a simplistic materialism, is dialectically justified by the perception that potentiality and its latent possibilities form an existential continuum that constitutes the authentic world of truth—the world of the "what-should-be," not simply the world of the "what-is," with all its incompleteness and falsehood.

From a dialectical viewpoint, a change in a given level of biotic, communal, or for that matter, social organization consists not simply of the appearance of a new, possibly more complex ensemble of "feedback loops." Rather, it consists of qualitatively new attributes, interrelationships, and degrees of subjectivity that express and radically condition the emergence of a new potentiality, opening up a new realm of possibility with its own unique tendency—not a greater or lesser number of "fluctuations" and "rhythms." Moreover, this new potentiality is itself the result of other actualizations of potentialities that, taken together historically and cumulatively, constitute a developmental continuum—not a bullet "shot from a pistol" that explodes into Being without a history of its own or a continuum of which it is part.[25]

Dialectical logic is an immanent logic of process—an *ontological* logic, not only a logic of concepts, categories, and symbols. This logic is emergent, in the sense that one speaks of the "logic of events." Considered in terms of its emphasis on differentiation, this logic is provocatively concrete in its relationship to abstract generalizations—hence Hegel's seemingly paradoxical expression "concrete universal." Dialectic thereby overcomes Plato's dualistic separation of exemplary ideas from the phenomenal world of imperfect "copies"—hence its ethical thrust is literally structured, cumulatively as well as sequentially, in the concrete. Emerging from this superb ensemble is a world that is always ethically problematical but also an ethics that is always objective, a recognition of selfhood and subjectivity that embodies nonhuman and human nature, and a development from metabolic self-maintenance to rational self-direction and innovation that locates the origins of reason *within* nature, not in a supramundane domain *apart* from nature. The social is thus wedded to the natural, and human reason is wedded to nonhuman subjectivity through processes that are richly mediated and graded in a shared continuum of development. This ecological interpretation of dialectic not only overcomes dualism but moves through differentiation away from reductionism.

Ecology cleanses the remarkable heritage of European organismic thought of the hard teleological predeterminations it acquired from Greek theology, the Platonistic denigration of physicality, and the Christian preoccupation with human inwardness as "soul" and a reverence for God. Only ecology can ventilate the dialectic as an orientation toward the objective world by rendering it coextensive with natural evolution, a possibility that arose in the last century with the appearance of evolutionary theory.

As such, an ecological dialectic is not solely a way of thinking organically; it can be a source of *meaning* to natural evolution—of *ethical* meaning, not only rational meaning. To state this idea more provocatively: we cannot hope to find humanity's "place in nature" without knowing how it *emerged* from nature, with all its problems and possibilities. An ecological dialectic produces a creative paradox: second nature in an ecological society would be the actualization of first nature's potentiality to achieve mind and truth. Human intellection in an ecological society would thus "fold back" upon the evolutionary continuum that exists in first nature. In this sense—and in this sense alone—second nature would thus become first nature rendered self-reflexive, a thinking nature that would know itself and could guide its own evolution, not an unthinking nature that "sought its own balance" through the "dynamics" of "fluc-tuations" and "feedback" that cause needless pain, suffering, and death. Although thought, society, and culture would retain their integrity, they would consciously express the abiding tendency within first nature to press itself toward the level of conscious self-directiveness.

In a very real sense, an ecological society would be *a transcendence of both first nature and second nature* into a new domain of a "free nature," a nature that in a truly rational humanity reached the level of conceptual thought—in short, a nature that would willfully and thinkingly cope with conflict, contingency, waste, and compulsion. In this new synthesis, where first and second nature are melded into a free, rational, and ethical nature, neither first nor second would lose its specificity and integrity. Humanity, far from diminishing the in-tegrity of nature, would add the dimension of freedom, reason, and ethics to it and raise evolution to a level of self-reflexivity that has always been latent in the emergence of the natural world.

To deny the potentiality for this transcendence and synthesis of first and second nature into a free nature is to leave ecological thinking open to all the wayward "if-then" propositions that threaten to overrun and brutalize it. Commonsense "brainstorms," throwing ideas into the air with a prayer that mere probability will provide us with a meaningful pattern, would replace reflection and intellectual exploration.

Today, the results of this desystematized thinking are often ludicrous when they are not simply cruel or even vicious. If all organisms in the biosphere are "intrinsically" equally "worthy" of a "right" to "self-realization," as many biocentrists believe, then human beings have no right, *given the full logic of this proposition,* to try to stamp out mosquitoes that carry malaria and yellow fever. Nor does the logic of this proposition give humanity the right to eliminate the AIDS virus or other organic sources of deadly illness.[26] It hardly helps that Bill Devall and George Sessions, the coauthors of *Deep Ecology,* hedged "biocentric equality" with the qualifier that "we have no right to destroy other living beings without sufficient reason."[27] A loophole like "sufficient reason" is ambiguous enough to divest the entire phrase of its logical integrity. Logic, in fact, gives way to a purely relativistic ethics. What Devall and Sessions consider "insufficient reason" to take a life may be very sufficient to many other people whose well-being, indeed whose very survival under the present "system" depends on it. In this kind of argumentation, which divests ethics of its social basis and second nature of its derivation from first nature, "centricity" bifurcates into two opposing bodies of values: a biocentrism that makes humans and viruses equal "citizens" in a "biospheric democracy," and an anthropocentrism that makes humans into self-centered sovereigns in what is presumably a biospheric tyranny. That both views are in error is a central point in this work. In any case, "deep ecology," taken at its word, leads us into a foggy and dangerous logical realm from which there is usually no recourse but Eastern mysticism.[28]

There is no "biospheric democracy"—or "tyranny," for that matter—in nature other than what human second nature imputes to nonhuman first nature, just as there is no hierarchy, domination, class structure, or state in the natural world—only what the socially conditioned human mind projects onto nonhuman biological relationships.

"Rights," in any meaningful sense of the word, are the product of custom, tradition, institutional development, and social relationships, of an increasingly self-conscious historical experience, and of *mind*—that is, conceptual thought that painstakingly formulates a constellation of rights and duties that makes for an empathetic respect for individuals and collectivities. They emerge from the human *social* sphere and from ways in which human communities *institutionalize* themselves. Leopards claim no "rights" for themselves and certainly recognize no "right" to life, much less to "self-realization," in the animals on which they prey.

As mammals, these predators may be more self-aware than, say, frogs, because of their more complex neurological and sensory apparatus. Hence, they may be more subjective, even more rational in a dim way. But their range of conceptualization, from everything we know, is so limited, often so immediately focused on their own survival needs, that to impute ethical judgments involving "rights" to them is to be truly anthropomorphic, often without even knowing so. When biocentrists, antihumanists, and "deep ecologists" flagellate us with claims that life-forms have "rights" to life and "self-realization" that we, as humans, fail to recognize, they unknowingly participate in a hidden anthropomorphism that we bring to many forms of life. They work from within human ideas and feelings—indeed, the best that constitutes humanism—to incarnate "rights" and the notion of a "biospheric democracy" in first nature. A human empathy and sense of identification that yield a profound respect and sensitivity for the nonhuman world should not be confused with sophisticated ethical "rights" and a "democracy" that have moral and political meaning—that is, unless we are prepared to undermine the authentic social content of "rights" and "democracy" for human society and intellection. Ironically, if there is to be anything that approximates a "biospheric democracy" in the nonhuman world, it will be shaped by human empathy, which *presupposes* the rational and ecological intervention of human beings into the natural world. This would entail the infusion of human values into nature, and human mind into nonhuman subjectivity.[29]

Biocentrists and antihumanists can hardly have their cake and eat it too. Either humanity is a distinctive moral agent in the biosphere, that can practice an ecological stewardship of nature—or else it is "one" with the whole world of life and simply dissolves into it. If the latter is true, then human beings have a "biospheric right" to use the biosphere exclusively to suit their own ends, a "right" that cannot be denied any more than the leopard's "right" to kill and feast on its prey, albeit less "efficiently" than human beings. At this point, antihumanists may change the whole level of the argument by replying that the despoliation of the earth by plundering "humans" (whoever they may be) will ultimately boomerang on the human species. But this turns their argument into a pragmatic problem of a purely instrumental character, reduces a problem in morality to a problem in engineering new technological fixes and the deployment of mere human cunning. Nature thus reverts to a Darwinian jungle that is morally neutral at best or engaged in a duel between human cunning and animal mindlessness at worst.

On the other hand, if we understand that human beings are indeed moral agents because natural evolution confers upon them a clear responsibility toward the natural world, we cannot emphasize their unique attributes too strongly. For it is this unique ability to think conceptually and feel a deep empathy for the world of life that makes it possible for humanity to reverse the devastation it has inflicted on the biosphere and create a rational society. This implies not only that humanity, once it came into its own humanity as the actualization of its potentialities, *could* be a rational expression of nature's creativity and fecundity, but that human intervention into natural processes *could* be as creative as natural evolution itself.

This evolutionary and dialectical viewpoint, which derives the human species from nature as the embodiment of nature's own thrust toward self-reflexivity, changes the entire argument around competing "rights" between human and nonhuman life-forms into an exploration of the *ways* in which human beings intervene into the biosphere. Whether humanity recognizes that an ecological society would be the fulfillment of a major tendency in natural evolution, or remains blind to its own humanity as a moral and ecological agent in nature, becomes a *social* problem that requires a *social* ecology. The self-effacing quietism and "spirituality" so rampant today afflict a sizable, highly privileged sector of Euro-

American society—human types so consumed by a "love" of nature and life that they may well ignore the needless but very real suffering and pain that exist in nature and society alike.

NOTES

1. This essay was originally published in *Our Generation*, vol. 18, no. 2 (Spring-Summer 1987). It has been revised for publication here.

2. This basically Marxian thesis, which all members of the Frankfurt School took for granted, is repeatedly misinterpreted, particularly in the ecology movement, when it is discussed at all. However much they opposed domination, neither Adorno nor Horkheimer singled out hierarchy as an underlying problematic in their writings. Indeed, their residual Marxian premises led to a historical fatalism that saw any liberatory enterprise (beyond art, perhaps) as hopelessly tainted by the need to dominate nature and *consequently* "man." This position stands completely at odds with my own view that the notion—and no more than an *unrealizable* notion—of dominating nature stems from the domination of human by human. This is not a semantic difference in accounting for the origins of domination. Like Marx, the Frankfurt School saw nature as a "domineering" force over humanity that human guile—and class rule—had to exorcise before a classless society was possible. The Frankfurt School, no less than Marxism, placed the onus for domination primarily on the demanding forces of nature.

   My own writings radically reverse this very traditional view of the relationship between society and nature. I argue that the idea of dominating nature first arose within *society* as part of its institutionalization into gerontocracies that placed the young in varying degrees of servitude to the old and in patriarchies that placed women in varying degrees of servitude to men—not in any endeavor to "control" nature or natural forces. Various modes of social institutionalization, not modes of organizing human labor (so crucial to Marx), were the first sources of domination, which is not to deny Marx's thesis that class society was economically exploitative. Hence, domination can be definitively removed only by resolving problematics that have their origins in hierarchy and status, not in class and the technological control of nature alone.

3. Leon E. Stover, *The Cultural Ecology of Chinese Civilization* (New York: Pica Press, 1974).

4. It is a compelling commentary on their naïveté that Westerners can so readily ignore oriental despotism in favor of a romantic reverence for Asian "sages." Chinese elites perfected an exquisitely cruel ethos toward the masses, whom they not only exploited physically but degraded spiritually. That this peasantry quietistically bent its head to the yoke does not speak well for Chinese "sages." The Tao Te Ching is an eminent-

ly political collection of passages. From the viewpoint of social ecology—which pointedly studies the *social* origins of a nature ideology and explores its logic—the passivity toward nature that the Tao Te Ching fostered could easily have been transposed into society, just as nature philosophy in the West has served social elites in the worst of cases, and rebels in the best. In any case, in 1989 Chinese students exhibited more interest in Western than Eastern ideals: they invoked ideals more redolent of the French Revolution than the Tao Te Ching by taking to the streets with demands for democracy and human rights.

5. Fritjof Capra, The Turning Point (New York: Simon and Schuster, 1982), pp. 286-87.

6. *Ibid.*, pp. 287, 412.

7. *Ibid.*, p. 288.

8. *Ibid.*

9. See Ilya Prigogine and Isabelle Stengers, *Order Out of Chaos* (New York: Bantam Books, 1984), pp. 291-310. The notion of the irreversibility of time, appropriate as it may be for Prigogine to emphasize it in order to exorcise a mechanistic dynamics based on time's reversibility, is not congruent with process and evolution; it is merely one presupposition of these phenomena.

10. That such cosmic formulas cannot explain the foundations of either organic or social development is not an argument against "foundationalism"—that is, the view that there are explanations that can account for differentiae in the biological and social as well as the inorganic physical world. Our world has more coherence than many relativists today are willing to admit, with its different levels of unfolding and, in their scope, different foundations, degrees of possibility, subjectivity and, with humanity, reason.

11. Capra, *Turning Point*, p. 288.

12. *Ibid.*, pp. 300, 393.

13. Gregory Bateson, *Mind and Nature* (New York: E.P. Dutton, 1979), p. 31.

14. For a more complete discussion of nature's fecundity and its source in species variety, see my "Freedom and Necessity in Nature," elsewhere in this book.

15. Human self-hatred, I may add, is not a psychological phenomenon alone; it has ugly social roots. The privileged hate not other privileged but the underprivileged, generally accusing them of "anthropocentric" vices and subjecting them to the constraints of "natural law."

16. David Foreman, interviewed by Bill Devall, "A Spanner in the Woods," *Simply Living*, vol. 12 (c. 1986).

17. Let me make it clear that I believe that nature is neither hierarchical nor egalitarian—concepts that are meaningless unless they are institutionalized socially, which presupposes a *human* presence in the biosphere, or second nature. What we encounter in first nature is *complementarity,* the mutualistic interaction of life-forms in maintaining a nonhuman ecological community. At this biological level, complementarity is not an ethics—which is associated with reasoned behavior—but a descriptive datum related to mutualism. I used the word *complementarity* to denote an ethics in *The Ecology of Freedom.* Since that book was published, "natural law" devotees have picked up on it with minimal acknowledgment and turned it into a "law of complementarity"—a regressive use of the concept if there ever was one.

18. I am not speaking about "dialectical materialism," which, whatever the intentions of Marx and Engels, used Hegelian terms and concepts to formulate what was little more than a scientistic "dialectical" mechanism. My purpose is not to flesh out the skeleton of dialectical philosophy with "materialism" or a latter-day nominalist physicality, but to bring nature into the foreground of dialectical thought in an evolutionary and organismic way.

19. G.R.G. Mure, *Aristotle* (New York: Oxford University Press, 1964), p. 7.

20. It is arguable whether Hegel saw teleology as an inflexible predetermination of the development of the "real" in its beginnings. Hegel's *Logic* exists on a different level from the existential reality we experience in history and everyday life. Its "purified" categories are developed from each other with a "logical necessity" and, in a metaphoric sense, could be seen as a rational level parallel to the existential level from which they are abstracted. This *logos,* as it were, could be taken as an exemplary and thus inherently critical vision of the world in a highly subjectivized form whose "logic" yields a distinct rational conclusion, just as Plato's domain of forms has been regarded by many Platonists as exemplary in a *normative* sense, as distinguished from the flawed world that we experience around us.

21. Responsibility for the confusion about the meaning of the words *real* and *actual* is by no means Hegel's but rather that of some of his translators. The German word *wirklich* has a family of English meanings that include "real" as well as "actual." Hegel was quite scrupulous in distinguishing the "real" from the "actual" in his *Science of Logic,* where "reality," as he put it in his discussion of "Determinate Being," seems "to be an ambiguous word," while "Actuality is the unity of Essence and Existence." See the Johnston and Struthers translation, *Science of Logic* (New York: Macmillan, 1929), vol. 1, p. 124, and vol. 2, p. 160. The problem arose when Hegel's famous maxim, *Was vernünftig ist, das ist wirklich; und was wirklich*

ist, das ist vernünftig, was mistranslated as "What is rational is real, and what is real is rational." The correct and philosophically meaningful translation is "What is rational is actual, and what is actual is rational." The mistranslation, which rendered *real* and *actual* synonyms, conceived the Hegelian *real* as the actualization of the potential. The mischief this mistranslation produced in the interpretation of Hegel's ideas is matched only by the confusion it produced in the interpretation of the maxim itself. Engels, ironically, clarified Hegel's meaning wonderfully—albeit using *real* rather than *actual.* See his *Ludwig Feuerbach and the End of German Philosophy,* in Marx and Engels, *Selected Works* (Moscow: Progress Publishers, 1970), vol. 3, pp. 337-38. I am not nitpicking here: the odium that Hegelian philosophy acquired as an apologia for the Prussian state rests in no small part on the failure to properly interpret—and translate— this famous maxim in Hegel's *Encyclopedia Logic* and *Philosophy of Right.*

22. G.W.F. Hegel, *Lectures on the History of Philosophy* (New York: Humanities Press, 1955), vol. 1, p. 22 (my emphasis). Here Hegel is describing the dialectic in unknowing nature. "In Mind it is otherwise," he is quick to add; "it is consciousness and therefore it is free, uniting in itself the beginning and the end—that is to say, intention, striving, and predetermination" (p. 22). In fact, from my viewpoint the conclusion that "Mind" is "free" could also mean that knowing beings can be wayward, idiosyncratic and one-sided, and—unlike nonhuman beings—cruel and, put bluntly, evil.

23. Unfortunately, this has not been noticed in most commentaries on Hegel's oeuvre, much less in philosophy generally, which seems more occupied with establishing what Heidegger means by "Being" than with other concepts of Being in Western thought.

24. "What-*could*-be," insofar as it involves organic subjectivity and flexibility, derives from the natural realm of potentiality. "What-*should*-be," the unfolding of the rational, is an ethical extrapolation of individual and social potentialities, of attributes of the truly self-determining person and society.

25. Viewed from this standpoint, there is a sense in which Hegel's "objective idealism" was more objective than his materialist critics realized. Possibilities—that is, the actualizations of existential potentialities—are as objective as the inherence of an oak tree in an acorn. Ethically, this highly illuminating approach establishes a standard of fulfillment—an objective good, as it were—that literally informs the existential with a goal of objective fulfillment, just as we say in everyday life that an individual who does not "live up" to his or her capabilities is an "unfulfilled" person and, in a sense, a less than "real" person.

26. Antihumanist "ethicists" actually take this argument seriously, I have been startled to learn. In biocentric ethics, reports Bernard Dixon, no "logical line can be drawn" between the conservation of whales, gentians, and flamingoes on the one hand and the conservation of pathogenic microbes like the smallpox virus on the other, which, according to one antihumanist wag (David Ehrenfeld), is "an endangered species." Logical consistency requires that we try to rescue the smallpox virus with the same ethical dedication that we bring to the survival of whales. See Bernard Dixon, "Smallpox—Imminent Extinction, and an Unresolved Problem," *New Scientist*, vol. 69 (1976). For an antihumanist position that verges on sheer misanthropy, see David Ehrenfeld, *The Arrogance of Humanism* (New York: Oxford University Press, 1978).

27. Bill Devall and George Sessions, *Deep Ecology* (Salt Lake City: Peregrine Smith Books, 1985), p. 67.

28. Or else by regarding the human condition with ugly indifference. Misanthropy, indeed an *inhumanity*, labeled biocentrism, "deep ecology," or population control, could provide a brutal mandate for human suffering and authoritarian state control. Ecology, on these terms, threatens to become an ideology that is cruel, not sharing or cooperative.

29. The more one examines the literature of biocentrists, antihumanists, and "deep ecologists," the more one senses manipulation. Their appeals to human feelings like empathy and identification are translated into "rights" that rest heavily on the historical development of humanism. Humanism involves not simply a claim to humanity's "superiority" over the nonhuman world but, significantly, an appeal to human reason and a social ethics of cooperation. Great social movements, uprisings, and ideologies, not to speak of self-sacrificing individuals, were committed to the achievement of these monumental goals—a history that is simply effaced from much of the biocentrist, antihumanist, and "deep ecology" literature. Often, their place is taken by a nagging denigration of the human spirit, decorated with metaphors lifted from Eastern philosophy. Social analysis tends to be minimized and even deflected by a privileged and inward concern with abstractions like "interconnectedness" and "oneness"—in a society riven by genuine conflicts between rich and poor, privileged and denied, and man and woman, not to speak of "deep," "deeper," and the "deepest" ecologists.

HISTORY, CIVILIZATION, AND PROGRESS
Outline for a Criticism of Modern Relativism

I

Rarely have the concepts that literally define the best of Western culture—its notions of a meaningful History, a universal Civilization, and the possibility of Progress—been called so radically into question as they are today. In recent decades, both in the United States and abroad, the academy and a subculture of self-styled postmodernist intellectuals have nourished an entirely new ensemble of cultural conventions that stem from a corrosive social, political, and moral relativism. This ensemble encompasses a crude nominalism, pluralism, and skepticism, an extreme subjectivism, and even outright nihilism and antihumanism in various combinations and permutations, sometimes of a thoroughly misanthropic nature. This relativistic ensemble is pitted against coherent thought as such and against the "principle of hope" (to use Ernst Bloch's expression) that marked radical theory of the recent past. Such notions percolate from so-called radical academics into the general public, where they take the form of personalism, amoralism, and "neoprimitivism."

Too often in this prevailing "paradigm," as it is frequently called, eclecticism replaces the search for historical meaning; a self-indulgent despair replaces hope; dystopia replaces the promise of a rational society; and in the more sophisticated forms of this ensemble a vaguely defined "intersubjectivity"—or in its cruder forms, a primitivistic mythopoesis—replaces all forms of reason, particularly dialectical reason. In fact, the very concept of reason itself has been challenged by a willful antirationalism. By stripping the great traditions of Western thought of their contours, nuances, and gradations, these relativistic "post-historicists," "postmodernists," and (to coin a new word) "post-humanists" of our day are, at best, condemning contemporary thought to a dark pessimism or, at worst, subverting it of all its meaning.

So grossly have the current critics of History, Civilization, and Progress, with their proclivities for fragmentation and reductionism, subverted the coherence of these basic Western concepts that they will literally have to be defined again if they are to be made intelligible to present and future generations. Even more disturbingly, such critics have all but abandoned attempts to define the very concepts they excoriate. What, after all, is *History*? Its relativistic critics tend to dissolve the concept into eclectically assembled "histories" made up of a multiplicity of disjointed episodes—or even worse, into myths that belong to "different" gender, ethnic, and national groups and that they consider to be ideologically equatable. Its nominalistic critics see the past largely as a series of "accidents," while its subjectivistic critics overemphasize ideas in determining historical realities, consisting of "imaginaries" that are essentially discontinuous from one another. And what, after all, is *Civilization*? "Neo-primitivists" and other cultural reductionists have so blackened the word that its rational components are now in need of a scrupulous sorting out from the irrationalities of the past and present. And what, finally, is *Progress*? Relativists have rejected its aspirations to freedom in all its complexity, in favor of a fashionable assertion of "autonomy," often reducible to personal proclivities. Meanwhile, antihumanists have divested the very concept of Progress of all relevance and meaning in the farrago of human self-denigration that marks the mood of the present time.

A skepticism that denies any meaning, rationality, coherence, and continuity in History, that corrodes the very existence of premises, let alone the necessity of exploring them, renders discourse itself virtually impossible. Indeed, premises as such have become so suspect that the new relativists regard any attempts to establish them as evidence of a cultural pathology, much as Freudian analysts might view a patient's resistance to treatment as symptomatic of a psychological pathology. Such a psychologization of discussion closes off all further dispute. No longer are serious challenges taken on their own terms and given a serious response; rather, they are dismissed as symptoms of a personal and social malaise.

So far have these tendencies been permitted to proceed that one cannot now mount a critique of incoherence, for ex-. ample, without exposing oneself to the charge of a having a "predisposition" to "coherence"—or a "Eurocentric" bias. A defense of clarity, equally unacceptable, invites the accusation of reinforcing the "tyranny of reason," while an attempt to uphold the validity of reason is dismissed as an "oppressive" presupposition of reason's existence. The very attempt at definition is rejected as intellectually "coercive." Rational discussion is impugned as a repression of nonliterate forms of "expression" such as rituals, howling, and dancing, or on an ostensibly philosophical scale, of intuitions, presciences, psychological motivations, of "positional" insights that are dependent on one's gender or ethnicity, or of revelations of one kind or another that often feed into outright mysticism.

This constellation of relativistic views, which range from the crude to the intellectually exotic, cannot be criticized rationally because they deny the validity of rationally independent conceptual formulations as such, presumably "constricted" by the claims of reason. For the new relativists, "freedom" ends where claims to rationality begin—in marked contrast to the ancient Athenians, for whom violence began where rational discussion ended. Pluralism, the decentering of meanings, the denial of foundations, and the hypostasization of the idiosyncratic, of the ethically and socially contingent, and of the psychological—all seem like part of the massive cultural decay that corresponds to the objective decay of our era. In American universities today, relativists in all their mutations too often retreat into the leprous "limit experiences" of Foucault; into a view of History as fragmentary "collective representations" (Durkheim), "culture-patterns" (Benedict), or "imaginaries" (Castoriadis); or into the nihilistic asociality of postmodernism.

When today's relativists do offer definitions of the concepts they oppose, they typically overstate and exaggerate them. They decry the pursuit of foundations—an endeavor that they have characteristically turned into an "ism," "foundationalism"—as "totalistic," without any regard for the patent need for basic principles. That foundations exist that are confined to *areas of reality where their existence is valid and knowable* seems to elude these antifoundationalists, for whom foundations must either encompass the entire cosmos or else not exist at all. Reality would indeed be a mystery if a few principles or foundations could encompass all that exists, indeed, all its innovations unfolding from the subatomic realm to inorganic matter, from the simplest to the most complex life-forms, and ultimately to the realm of astrophysics.

Some historical relativists overemphasize the subjective in history at the expense of the material. Subjective factors certainly do affect obviously objective developments. In the Hellenistic Age, for example, Heron reputedly designed steam engines, yet so far as we know they were never used to replace human labor, as they were two thousand years later. Subjective historians, to be sure, would emphasize the subjective factors in this fact. But what *interaction* between ideological and material factors explains why one society—capitalism—used the steam engine on a vast scale for the manufacture of commodities, while another—Hellenistic society—used it merely to open temple doors for the purposes of mass mystification? Overly subjectivistic historians would do well to explore not only how different traditions and sensibilities yielded these disparate uses of machines but what *material* as well as broadly social factors either fostered or produced them.[1]

Other historical relativists are nominalistic, overemphasizing the idiosyncratic in History, often begging basic questions that must be explored. A small group of people in ancient Judea, we may be told, formulated a localized, ethnically based body of monotheistic beliefs that at a chronologically later point became the basis of the Judeo-Christian world religion. Are these two events unrelated? Was their conjunction a mere accident? To conceive this vast development in a nominalistic way, without probing into *why* the Roman emperors adopted the Judeo-Christian synthesis—in an empire composed of very different cultures and languages that was direly in need of ideological unity to prevent its complete collapse—is to produce confusion rather than clarity.

Perhaps the most problematic aspect of relativism is its moral arbitrariness. The moral relativism of the trite maxim "What's good for me is good for me, and what's good for you is good for you," hardly requires elucidation.[2] In this apparently most formless of times, relativism has left us with a solipsistic morality and in certain subcultures a politics literally premised on chaos. The turn of many anarchists these days toward a highly personalistic, presumably "autonomous" subculture at the expense of responsible social commitment and action reflects, in my view, a tragic abdication of a serious engagement in the political and revolutionary spheres. This is no idle problem today, when increasing numbers of people with no knowledge of History take capitalism to be a natural, eternal social system. A politics rooted in purely relativistic preferences, in assertions of personal "autonomy" that stem largely from an individual's "desire," can yield a crude and self-serving opportunism, of a type whose prevalence today explains many social ills. Capitalism itself, in fact, fashioned its primary ideology on an equation of freedom with the personal autonomy of the individual, which Anatole France once impishly described as the "freedom" of everyone to sleep at night under the same bridge over the Seine. Individuality is *inseparable* from community, and autonomy is hardly meaningful unless it is embedded in a cooperative community.[3] Compared with humanity's potentialities for freedom, a relativistic and personalistic "autonomy" is little more than psychotherapy writ large and expanded into a social theory.

Far too many of the relativistic critics of History, Civilization, and Progress seem less like serious social theorists than like frightened former radical ideologues who have not fully come to terms with the failures of the Left and of "existing socialism" in recent years. The incoherence that is celebrated in present-day theory is due in no small part to the one-sided and exaggerated reaction of French academic "leftists" to the May-June events of 1968, to the behavior of the French Communist Party, and in even greater part to the various mutations of Holy Mother Russia from Tsarism through Stalinism to Yeltsinism. Too often, this disenchantment provides an escape route for erstwhile "revolutionaries" to ensconce themselves in the academy, to embrace social democracy, or simply to turn to a vacuous nihilism that hardly constitutes a threat to the existing society. From relativism, they have constructed a skeptical barrier between themselves and the rest of society. Yet this barrier is as intellectually fragile as the one-sided absolutism that the Old Left tried to derive from Hegel, Marx, and Lenin.

Fairness requires me to emphasize that contrary to the conventional wisdom about the Left today, there has never been any "existing socialism," the erstwhile claims of Eastern European leaders to have achieved it notwithstanding. Nor was Hegel a mere teleologist; nor Marx a mere "productivist"; nor Lenin the ideological "father" of the ruthless opportunist and counterrevolutionary, Stalin.[4] In reaction to the nightmare of the "Soviet" system, today's relativists have not only overreacted to and exaggerated the shortcomings of Hegel, Marx, and Lenin; they have concocted an ideological prophylaxis to protect themselves from the still-unexorcised demons of a tragically failed past instead of formulating a credible philosophy that can address the problems that now confront us at all levels of society and thought.

Current expositions of oxymoronic "market socialisms" and "minimal statisms" by "neo-" and "post-Marxists" suggest where political relativism and assertions of "autonomy" can lead us.[5] Indeed, it is quite fair to ask whether today's fashionable political relativism itself would provide us with more than a paper-thin obstacle to totalitarianism. The dismissal of attempts to derive continuity in History, coherence in Civilization, and meaning in Progress as evidence of a "totalizing" or "totalitarian" mentality in pursuit of all-encompassing foundations directly or indirectly imbricates reason, particularly that of the Enlightenment era, with totalitarianism, and even significantly *trivializes* the harsh reality and pedigree of totalitarianism itself. In fact, the actions of the worst totalitarians of our era, Stalin and Hitler, were guided less by the objectively grounded principles or "foundational" ideas they so cynically voiced in public than by a kind of relativistic or situational ethics. For Stalin, who was no more a "socialist" or "communist" than he was an "anarchist" or "liberal," theory was merely an ideological fig leaf for the concentration of power. To overlook Stalin's sheer opportunism is myopic at best and cynical at worst. Under his regime, only a hopelessly dogmatic "Communist" who had managed to negotiate and survive Stalin's various changes in the "party line" could have taken Stalin seriously as a "Marxist-Leninist." Hitler, in turn, exhibited amazing flexibility in bypassing ideology for strictly pragmatic ends. In his first months in power, he decimated all the "true believers" of National Socialism among his storm troopers at the behest of the Prussian officer caste, which feared and detested the Nazi rabble.

In the absence of an objective grounding—notably, the very real human potentialities that have been formed by the natural, social, moral, and intellectual development of our species—notions like freedom, creativity, and rationality are reduced to "intersubjective" relations, underpinned by personal and individualistic preferences (nothing more!) that are "resolved" by another kind of tyranny—notably, the tyranny of consensus. Lacking foundations of any kind, lacking any real form and solidity, notions of "intersubjectivity" can be frighteningly homogenizing because of their seemingly "democratic" logic of consensuality—a logic that precludes the dissensus and ideological dissonance so necessary for stimulating innovation. In the consensual "ideal speech situation" that Jürgen Habermas deployed to befog the socialist vision of the 1970s, this "intersubjectivity," a transcendental "Subject" or "Ego" like a mutated Rousseauian "General Will," replaces the rich elaboration of reason. Today this subjectivism or "intersubjectivity"—be it in the form of Habermas's neo-Kantianism or Baudrillard's egoism—lends itself to a notion of "social theory" as a matter of personal taste. Mere constructions of "socially conditioned" human minds, free-floating in a sea of relativism and ahistoricism, reject a potential objective ground for freedom in the interests of avoiding "totalitarian Totalities" and the "tyranny" of an "Absolute." Indeed, *reason itself* is essentially reduced to "intersubjectivity." Juxtaposed with literary celebrations of the "subjective reason" of personalism, and its American sequelae of mysticism, individual redemption, and conformity, and its post-1968 French sequelae of postmodernist, psychoanalytic, relativist, and neo-Situationist vagaries, Marx's commitment to thorough thinking would be attractive.

Ideas that are objectively grounded, unlike those that are relativistically asserted, can provide us with a *definable* body of principles with which we can seriously grapple. The foundational coherence and, in the best of cases, the rationality of objectively grounded views at least make them explicit and tangible and free them from the vagaries of the labyrinthine personalism so very much in vogue today. Unlike a foundationless subjectivism that is often reducible, under the rubric of "autonomy," to personal preferences, objective foundations are at least subject to challenges in a *free* society. Far from precluding rational critique, they invite it. Far from taking refuge in an unchallengeable nominalist elusiveness, they open themselves to the test of coherence. Paul Feyerabend's corrosive (in my view, cynical) relativism to the contrary notwithstanding, the natural sciences in the past three centuries have been among the most emancipatory human endeavors in the history of ideas—partly because of their pursuit of unifying or foundational explanations of reality.[6] In the end, what should always be of concern to us is the *content* of objective principles, be they in science, social theory, or ethics, not a flippant condemnation of their claims to coherence and objectivity per se.

Indeed, despite claims to the contrary, relativism has its own hidden "foundations" and metaphysics. As such, because its premises are masked, it may well produce an ideological tyranny far more paralyzing than the "totalitarianism" that it imputes to objectivism and an expressly *reasoned* "foundationalism." Insofar as our concerns should center on the *bases* of freedom and the *nature* of reason, modern relativism has "decentered" these crucial issues into wispy expressions of personal faith in an atmosphere of general skepticism. We may choose to applaud the relativist who upholds his or her strictly personal faith by reiterating Luther's defiant words at Worms, *Hier stehe ich, ich kann nicht anders* ("Here I stand, I cannot do otherwise"). But to speak frankly, unless we also hear a rational argument to validate that stand, one based on more than a subjective inclination, who gives a damn about this resolve?

II

Which again raises the problem of what History, Civilization, and Progress actually are.

History, I wish to contend, is the rational content and continuity of events (with due regard for qualitative "leaps") that are grounded in humanity's potentialities for freedom, self-consciousness, and cooperation, in the self-formative development of increasingly libertarian forms of consociation. It is the rational "infrastructure," so to speak, that coheres human actions and institutions over the past and the present in the direction of an emancipatory society and emancipated individuals. That is to say, History is precisely what is *rational* in human development. It is what is rational, moreover, in the *dialectical* sense of the implicit that unfolds, expands, and begins in varying degrees through increasing differentiation to actualize humanity's very *real* potentialities for freedom, self-consciousness, and cooperation.[7]

It will immediately be objected that irrational events, unrelated to this actualization, explode upon us at all times, in all eras and cultures. But insofar as they defy rational interpretation, they remain precisely *events*, not History, however consequential their effects may be on the course of other events. Their impact may be very powerful, to be sure, but they are not dialectically rooted in humanity's potentialities for freedom, self-consciousness, and cooperation.[8] They can be assembled into *Chronicles*, the stuff out of which Froissart constructed his largely anecdotal "histories," but not History in the sense I am describing. Events may even "overtake History," so to speak, and ultimately submerge it in the irrational and the evil. But without an increasingly self-reflexive History, which present-day relativism threatens to extinguish, we would not even know that it had happened.

If we deny that humanity has these potentialities for freedom, self-consciousness, and cooperation—conceived as one ensemble—then along with many self-styled "socialists" and even former anarchists like Daniel Cohn-Bendit, we may well conclude that "capitalism has won," as one disillusioned friend put it; that "history" has reached its terminus in "bourgeois democracy" (however tentative this "terminus" may actually be); and that rather than attempt to enlarge the realm of the rational and the free, we would do best to ensconce ourselves in the lap of capitalism and make it as comfortable a resting place as possible for ourselves.

As a mere adaptation to what exists, to the "what-is," such behavior is merely animalistic. Sociobiologists may even regard it as genetically unavoidable. But my critics need not be socio- biologists to observe that the historical record exhibits a great deal of adaptation and worse—of irrationality and violence, of pleasure in the destruction of oneself and others—and to ques- tion my assertion that History is the unfolding of human poten- tialities for freedom, self-consciousness, and cooperation. Indeed, humans have engaged in destruction and luxuriated in real and imaginary cruelties toward one another that have produced hells on earth. They have created the monstrosities of Hitler's death camps and Stalin's gulags, not to speak of the mountains of skulls that Mongol and Tartar invaders of Eurasia left behind in distant centuries. But this record hardly supplants a dialectic of unfolding and maturing of potentialities in social development, nor is the *capacity* of humans to inflict cruelties on each other equivalent to their *potentialities* for freedom, self-consciousness, and cooperation.

Here, human capacities and human potentialities must be distinguished from each other. The human capacity for inflicting injury belongs to the realm of natural history, to what humans share with animals in the biological world or "first nature." First nature is the domain of survival, of core feelings of pain and fear, and in that sense our behavior remains animalistic, which is by no means altered with the emergence of social or "second na- ture." *Unknowing* animals merely try to survive and adapt to one degree or another to the world in which they exist. By contrast, humans are animals of a very *special* kind; they are *knowing* animals, they have the intelligence to calculate and to devise, even in the service of needs that they share with nonhuman life-forms. Human reason and knowledge have commonly served aims of self-preservation and self-maximization by the use of a formal logic of expediency, a logic that rulers have deployed for social control and the manipulation of society. These methods have their roots in the animal realm of simple "means-ends" choices to survive.

But humans also have the *capacity* to *deliberately* inflict pain and fear, to use their reason for perverse passions, in order to coerce others or merely for cruelty for its own sake. Only *knowing* animals, ironically capable of intelligent innovation, with the *Schadenfreude* to enjoy vicariously the torment of others, can inflict fear and pain in a coldly calculated or even passionate manner. The Foucauldian hypostasization of the body as the "terrain" of sado-masochistic pleasure can be easily elaborated into a metaphysical justification of violence, depending, to be sure, on what "pleases" a particular perpetrating ego.[9] In this sense, human beings are too intelligent *not* to live in a rational society, *not* to live within institutions formed by reason and ethics that restrict their capacity for irrationality and violence.[10] Insofar as they do not, humans remain dangerously wayward and unformed creatures with enormous powers of destruction as well as creation.

Humanity may have a "potentiality for evil," as one colleague has argued. But that over the course of social development people have exhibited an explosive capacity to perpetrate the most appallingly evil acts does not mean that human potentiality is constituted to produce evil and a nihilistic destructiveness. The capacity of certain Germans to establish an Auschwitz, indeed the means and the goal to exterminate a whole people in a terrifyingly industrial manner, was inherent neither in Germany's development nor in the development of industrial rationalization as such. However anti-Semitic many Germans were over the previous two centuries, Eastern Europeans were equally or even more so; ironically, industrial development in Western Europe may have done more to achieve Jewish juridical emancipation in the nineteenth and twentieth centuries than all the Christian pieties that marked preindustrial life during the Middle Ages. Indeed, evil may have a "logic"—that is to say, it may be explained. But most general accounts explain the evolution of evil in terms of adventitious evil acts and events, if this can be regarded as explanation at all. Hitler's takeover of Germany, made possible more by economic and political dislocations than by the racial views he espoused, was precisely a terrible *event* that cannot be explained in terms of any human potentiality for evil. The horror of Auschwitz lies almost as much in its *inexplicability*, in its appallingly extraordinary character, as in the monstrosities that the Nazis generally inflicted on European Jews. It is in this sense that Auschwitz remains hauntingly *inhuman* and that it has tragically produced an abiding mistrust by many people of Civilization and Progress.

When explanations of evil are not merely narrations of events, they explain evil in terms of instrumental or conventional logic. The knowing animal, the human being, who is viciously harmful, does not use the developmental reason of dialectic, the reason of ethical reflection; nor a coherent, reflective reason, grounded in a knowledge of History and Civilization; nor even the knowing of an ambiguous, arbitrary, self-generated "imaginary," or a morality of personal taste and pleasure. Rather, the knowing animal uses instrumental calculation to serve evil ends, including the infliction of pain.

The very existence of irrationalism and evil in many social phenomena today compels us to uphold a clear standard of the "rational" and the "good" by which to judge the one against the other. A purely personalistic, relativistic, or functional approach will hardly do for establishing ethical standards—as many critiques of subjectivism and subjective reason have shown. The personal tastes from which subjectivism and relativism derive their ethical standards are as transient and fleeting as moods. Nor will a nominalistic approach suffice: to reduce History to an incomprehensible assortment of patterns or to inexplicable products of the imagination is to deny social development all internal *ethical* coherence.[11] Indeed, an unsorted, ungraded, unmediated approach reduces our understanding of History to a crude eclecticism rather than an insightful coherence, to an overemphasis on differentiae (so easy to do, these mindless days!) and the idiosyncratic rather than the meaningful and the universal, more often attracting the commonsensical individual to the psychoanalytic couch than helping him or her reconstitute a left libertarian social movement.

If our views of social development are to be structured around the *differences* that distinguish one culture or period from another, we will ignore underlying tendencies that, with extraordinary universality, have greatly expanded the material and cultural conditions for freedom on various levels of individual and social self-understanding. By grossly emphasizing disjunctions, social isolates, unique configurations, and chance events, we will reduce shared, clearly common social developments to an archipelago of cultures, each essentially unrelated to those that preceded and followed it. Yet many historical forces have emerged, declined, and emerged again, despite the formidable obstacles that often seemed to stand in their way. One does not have to explain "everything" in "foundational" terms to recognize the existence of *abiding* problems such as scarcity, exploitation, class rule, domination, and hierarchy that have agonized oppressed peoples for thousands of years.[12] If critics were correct in dubbing dialectic a mystery for claiming to encompass *all* phenomena by a few cosmic formulas, then they would be obliged to regard human social development as a mystery if they claimed that it lacks any continuity and unity—that is, the bases for a philosophy of History. Without a notion of continuity in History, how can we explain the extraordinary efflorescence of culture and technique that *Homo sapiens sapiens* produced during the Magdelenian period, some twenty or thirty thousand years ago? How can we explain the clearly unrelated evolution of complex agricultural systems in at least three separate parts of the world—the Middle East, Southeast Asia, and Mesoamerica—that apparently had no contact with one another and that were based on the cultivation of very different grains, notably wheat, rice, and maize? How can we explain the great gathering of social forces in which, after ten thousand years of arising, stagnating, and disappearing, cities finally gained control over the agrarian world that had impeded their development, yielding the "urban revolution," as V. Gordon Childe called it, in different areas of the world that could have had no contact with one another?

Mesoamerica and Mesopotamia, most clearly, could not have had any contact with each other since Paleolithic times, yet their agriculture, towns and cities, literacy, and mathematics developed in ways that are remarkably similar. Initially

Paleolithic foragers, both produced highly urbanized cultures based on grain cultivation, glyphs, accurate calendrics, and very elaborate pottery, to cite only the most striking parallels. The wheel was known to Mesoamericans, although they do not seem to have used it, probably for want of appropriate draft animals, as well as the zero, despite the absence of any communication with Eurasian societies. It requires an astonishing disregard for the unity of Civilization on the part of historical relativists to emphasize often minor differences, such as clothing, some daily customs, and myths, at the expense of a remarkable unity of consciousness and social development that the two cultures exhibited on two separate continents after many millennia of isolation from each other.

The unity of social evolution is hardly vitiated by such nominalistic perplexities as "Why didn't a Lenin appear in Germany rather than Russia in 1917-1918?" In view of the great *tidal* movements of History, it might be more appropriate to explore— Lenin's strong will and Kerensky's psychological flaccidity aside—whether the traditional proletariat was *ever* capable of creating a "workers' state," indeed, what that statist concept really meant when working men and women were obliged to devote the greater amount of their lives to arduous labor at the expense of their participation in managing social affairs. Caprice, accident, irrationality, and "imaginaries" certainly enter into social development for better or worse. But they literally have no meaning if there is no ethical standard by which to define the "other" of what we are presupposing with our standard.[13] Seemingly accidental or eccentric factors must be raised to the level of *social theory* rather than shriveled to the level of nominalistic minutiae if we are to understand them.

Despite the accidents, failures, and other aberrations that can alter the course of *rational* social and individual development, there is a *"legacy of freedom,"* as I named a key chapter in my book *The Ecology of Freedom,* a tradition of increasing approximation of humanity toward freedom and self-consciousness, in ideas and moral values and the overall terrain of social life. Indeed, the existence of History as a coherent unfolding of real emancipatory potentialities is clearly verified by the existence of *Civilization,* the potentialities of History embodied and partially actualized. It consists of the concrete advances, material as well as cultural and psychological, that humanity *has* made toward greater degrees of freedom, self-consciousness, and cooperation, as well as rationality itself. To have transcended the limitations of the kinship tie; to have gone beyond mere foraging into agriculture and industry; to have replaced the parochial band or tribe with the increasingly universal city; to have devised writing, produced literature, and developed richer forms of expression than non-literate peoples could have ever imagined—all of these and many more advances have provided the conditions for evolving increasingly sophisticated notions of individuality and expanding notions of reason that remain stunning achievements to this very day.

It is dialectical reason rather than conventional reason that apprehends the development of this tradition. Indeed, dialectical logic can hardly be treated coequally with eruptions of brutality, however calculated they may be, since in no sense can *episodic capacities* be equated with an *unfolding potentiality.* A dialectical understanding of History apprehends differentiae in quality, logical continuity, and maturation in historical development, as distinguished from the kinetics of mere change or a simple directivity of "social dynamics." Rarefying projects for human liberation to the point that they are largely subjective "imaginaries," without relevance to the realities of the overall human experience and the insights of speculative reason, can cause us to overlook the existential impact of these developments and the promise they hold for ever-greater freedom, self-consciousness, and cooperation. We take these achievements all too easily for granted without asking what kind of human beings we would be if they had not occurred as a result of historical and cultural movements more fundamental than eccentric factors. These achievements, let us acknowledge quite clearly, *are* Civilization, indeed a civilizing continuum that is nonetheless infused by terribly barbaric, indeed animalistic features. The civilizing process has been ambiguous, as I have emphasized in my "Ambiguities of Freedom,"14 but it has nonetheless historically turned folk into citizens, while the process of environmental adaptation that humans share with animals has been transformed into a wide-ranging, strictly human process of *innovation* in distinctly alterable environments.15 It is a process that reached its greatest universality *primarily* in Europe, however much other parts of the world have fed into the experience. Those of us who understandably fear that the barrier between Civilization and chaos is fragile actually *presuppose* the existence of Civilization, not simply of chaos, and the *existence* of rational coherence, not simply of irrational incoherence.

Moreover, the dialectic of freedom has emerged again and again in *recurring struggles for freedom,* ideological as well as physical, that have abidingly *expanded* overall goals of freedom, self-consciousness, and cooperation—as much in social evolution as a whole as within specific temporal periods. The past is replete with instances in which masses of people, however disparate their cultures, have tried to resolve the same millennia-old problems in remarkably similar ways and with remarkably similar views. The famous cry for equality that the English peasants raised in their 1381 revolt—"When Adam delved and Eve span, who was then the gentleman?"—is as meaningful for contemporary revolts as it was six hundred years ago, in a world that presumably had a far different "imaginary" from our own. The denial of a rational universal History, of Civilization, of Progress, and of social *continuity* renders any historical *perspective* impossible and hence any revolutionary praxis meaningless except as a matter of personal, indeed often *very* personal, taste.

Even as social movements attempt to attain what they might call a rational society, in developing humanity's potentialities for freedom, self-consciousness, and cooperation, History may constitute itself as an ever-developing "whole." This whole, I should emphasize, must be distinguished from a terminal Hegelian "Absolute," just as demands for coherence in a body of views must be distinguished from the worship of such an "Absolute" and just as the capacity of speculative reason to educe in a dialectically logical manner the *very real potentialities* of humanity for freedom is neither teleological nor absolutist, much less "totalitarian."[16] There is nothing teleological, mystical, or absolutist about History. "Wholeness" is no teleological referent, whose evolving components are merely parts of a predetermined "Absolute." Neither the rational unfolding of human potentialities nor their actualization in an eternally given "Totality" is predestined.

Nor is the working out of our potentialities some vague sort of suprahuman activity. Human beings are not the passive tools of a Spirit *(Geist)* that works out its complete and final self-realization and self-consciousness. Rather, they are *active agents,* the authentic "constituents" of History, who may or may not elaborate their potentialities in social evolution. Aborted the revolutionary tradition has been here, and discontinuous it has been there—and for all we know it may ultimately be aborted for humanity as such. Whether an "ultimate" rational society will even exist as a liberatory "end of history" is beyond anyone's predictive powers. We cannot say what the scope of a rational, free, and cooperative society would be, let alone presume to claim knowledge of its "limits." Indeed, insofar as the historical process effected by living human agents is likely to expand our notions of the rational, the democratic, the free, and the cooperative, it is undesirable to dogmatically assert that they have any finality. History forms its own ideal of these notions at various times, which in turn have been expanded and enriched.

Every society has the possibility of attaining a remarkable degree of rationality, given the material, cultural, and intellectual conditions that allow for it or, at least, are available to it. Within the limits of a slave, patriarchal, warrior, and urban world, for example, the ancient Athenian *polis* functioned *more* rationally than Sparta or other Greek *poleis.* It is precisely the task of speculative reason to educe *what should exist* at any given period, based on the very real potentialities for the expansion of these notions. To conclude that "the end of history" has been attained in liberal capitalism would be to jettison the historical legacy of these magnificent efforts to create a free society—efforts that claimed countless lives in the great revolutions of the past. For my part, I and probably many revolutionaries today want no place in such an "end of history"; nor do I want to forget the great emancipatory movements for popular freedom in all their many forms that occurred over the ages.

History, Civilization, and Progress are the *dialectically rational* social dispensations that form, even with all the impediments they face, a dialectical legacy of freedom. The existence of this legacy of freedom in no way denies the existence of a "legacy of domination,"[17] which remains within the realm of the irrational. Indeed, these "legacies" intertwine with and condition each other. Human ideals, struggles, and achievements of various approximations to freedom cannot be separated from the cruelties and barbarities that have marked social development over the centuries, often giving rise to new social configurations whose development is highly unpredictable. But a crucial historical problematic remains, to the extent that reason can foresee a given development: will it be freedom or domination that is nourished? I submit that *Progress* is the advance—and as everyone presumably hopes, the ascendancy—of freedom over domination, which clearly cannot be conceptually frozen in an ahistorical eternity, given the growing awareness of both hopes and oppressions that have come to light in only a few recent generations. Progress also appears in the overall improvement, however ambiguous, of humanity's material conditions of life, the emergence of a rational ethics, with enlightened standards of sensibility and conduct, out of unreflexive custom and theistic morality, and social institutions that foster continual self-development and cooperation. However lacking our ethical claims in relation to social practice may be, given all the barbarities of our time, we now subject brutality to much harsher judgments than was done in earlier times.

It is difficult to conceive of a rational ethics—as distinguished from unthinking custom and mere commandments of morality, like the Decalogue—without *reasoned* criteria of good and evil based on real potentialities for freedom that speculative reason can educe *beyond a given reality*. The "sufficient conditions" for an ethics must be explicated rationally, not simply affirmed in public opinion polls, plebiscites, or an "intersubjective" consensus that fails to clarify what constitutes "subjectivity" and "autonomy." Admittedly, this is not easy to do in a world that celebrates vaporous words, but it is necessary to discover truth rather than work with notions that stem from the conventional "wisdom" of our times. As Hegel insisted, even commonplace moral maxims like "Love thy neighbor as thyself" raise many problems, such as what we really mean by "love."[18]

III

I believe that we lack an adequate Left critique of the theoretical problems raised by classical Hegelianism, Marxism, anarchism, social democracy, and liberalism, with the result that there are serious lacunae in the critical exploration of these "isms." A comprehensive critical exploration would require an analysis not only of the failings of the subject matter under discussion, but of the hidden presuppositions of the critic. The critic would be obliged to clearly define what he or she *means* by the concepts he or she is using. This self-reflexive obligation cannot be bypassed by substituting undertheorized terms like "creativity," "freedom," and "autonomy" for in-depth analysis. The complexity of these ideas, their sweep, the traditions that underpin and divide them against one another, and the ease with which they can be abused and, in the academic milieux in which they are bandied around, detached from the lived material and social conditions of life—all require considerable exploration.

Among the important concepts and relationships that require elucidation is the tendency to reduce objectivity to the "natural law" of physical science.[19] In the conventional scientific sense of the term, "natural law" preordains the kinetic future of objects colliding with each other. It may even preordain what an individual plant will become under the normal conditions required for its growth. Objectivity, however, has a multiplicity of meanings and does not necessarily correspond to the "laws" that the natural sciences seek to formulate. It involves not only the materiality of the world in a broad sense but also its *potentialities,* as very real but as yet unrealized form structured to undergo elaboration. The evolution of key life-forms toward ever-greater subjectivity, choice, and behavioral flexibility—*real* potentialities and their degrees of actualization—and toward human intellectuality, language, and social institutionalization, is transparently clear. An objective potentiality is the *implicit* that may or may not be actualized, depending upon the conditions in which it emerges. Among humans, the actualization of potentiality is not *necessarily* restricted by anything besides aging and death, although it is not free to unfold unconditionally. Minimally, the actualization of humanity's potentialities consists in its attainment of a rational society. Such a society, of course, would not appear *ab novo*. By its very nature it would require development, maturation, or, more precisely, a History—a rational development that may be fulfilled by the very fact that the society *is* potentially constituted to be rational. If the self-realization of life in the nonhuman world is survival or stability, the self-realization of humanity is the degree of freedom, self-consciousness, and cooperation, as well as rationality in society. Reduced merely or primarily to scientific "natural law," objectivity is highly attenuated. It does not encompass potentiality and the working of the dialectic in existential reality, let alone its presence as a standard for gauging reality against actuality in the unfolding of human phenomena.[20]

Marx's claim to have unearthed "the natural laws of capitalist production" was absurd, but to advance relativism as an alternative to it is equally absurd. A younger, more flexible Marx insightfully claimed, "It is not enough that thought should seek its actualization; actuality itself must strive toward thought."[21] Thought, qua dialectical reason, becomes transformative in shaping the present and the future insofar as human rational praxis objectively actualizes the implicit. Today, when subjectivism reigns supreme and the common response even to significant events is to erase any meaning and coherence from History, Civilization, and Progress, there is a desperate need for an objectivity that is immensely broader than natural science and "natural laws," on the one hand, and an emphasis on the idiosyncratic, "imaginary," and adventitious, on the other. If vulgar Marxists used "science" to turn the *ethical* claim that "socialism is necessary" into the *teleological* assertion that "socialism is inevitable," today's "post-Marxist" critics repeat a similar vulgarity by mordantly celebrating incoherence in the realm of social theory. The claim of socialism's inevitability was crudely deterministic; the claim of its necessity was a rational and ethical explication.

"Intersubjectivity" and "intersubjective relations," for their part, cannot explain in any meaningful way *how* humanity is rooted in biological evolution, or what we broadly call "Nature," least of all by deftly using the phrase "social construction" to bypass the very objective evolutionary reality that "Nature" connotes. Just as a subjectivized nexus of "intersubjective relations" dissolves the objectivity of social phenomena, so a subjectivized nexus of "social construction" dissolves the objectivity of natural evolution, as if neither social phenomena nor natural evolution had any actuality, aside from being a pair of simplistic epistemological categories. Here Kant reappears with a vengeance, with the possible difference that even his noumenal or unknowable external reality has disappeared.

Dialectic, it should be emphasized, cannot be reduced merely to a "method" on the grounds that such disparate dialectical thinkers as Aristotle, John Scotus Eriugena, Hegel, and Marx comprehended different realms of knowledge and reality in different ways and periods. Humanity's knowledge of dialectic *has itself been a process*, and dialectical thinking has itself undergone development—a *cumulative* development, not a so-called "paradigm shift"—just as scientists have been obliged in the give-and-take or sublation of ideas to resolve one-sided insights into the nature of reality and its becoming.[22]

Although the broader objectivity that dialectical reasoning educes does not dictate that reason *will* prevail, it implies that it *should* prevail, thereby melding ethics with human activity and creating the basis for a truly objective ethical socialism or anarchism. As such, dialectic is not simply an ontological causality; *it is also an ethics*—an aspect of dialectical philosophy that has not been sufficiently emphasized. Dialectical reason permits an ethics in history by upholding the rational influence of "what-should-be" as against "what-is." History, qua the dialectically rational, exercises a pressing claim, so to speak, on our canons of behavior and our interpretation of events. Without this liberatory legacy and a human practice that fosters its unfolding, we have absolutely no basis for even *judging* what is creative or stagnant, rational or irrational, or good or evil in any constellation of cultural phenomena other than personal preference. Unlike science's limited objectivity, dialectical naturalism's objectivity is ethical *by its very nature,* by virtue of the kind of society it identifies as rational, a society that is the actualization of humanity's potentialities.[23] It sublates science's narrow objectivity to advance, by rational inferences drawn from the objective nature of human potentialities, a society that increasingly actualizes those potentialities. And it does so on the basis of what *should be* as the fulfillment of the rational, that is to say, on rational knowledge of the good and a conceptual congruence between the good and the socially rational that can be embodied in free institutions.

It is not that social development is dialectical because it is *necessarily* rational, as a traditional Hegelian might suppose, but rather that where social development *is* rational, it is dialectical or historical. We aver, in short, that we can educe from a uniquely human potentiality a rational development that advances human self-realization in a free, self-conscious, and cooperative society. Speculative reason here stakes out a claim to discern the rational development (by no means immune to irrational vicissitudes) of society as it *should be*—given human potentiality, as we know it in real life, to evolve from a tribal folk to a democratic citizenry, from mythopoesis to reason, from the submission of personhood in a folklike collectivity to individuality in a rational community—all as rational ends as well as existential realities. Speculative reason should always be called upon to understand and *explain* not only what has happened with respect to these problematics but *why* they recur in varying degrees and how they can be resolved.

In a very real sense, the past fifteen or more years have been remarkably *ahistorical*, albeit highly *eventful*, insofar as they have not been marked by any lasting advance toward a rational society. Indeed, if anything, they would seem to be tilting toward a regression, ideologically and structurally, to barbarism, despite spectacular advances in technology and science, whose outcome we cannot foresee. There cannot be a dialectic, however, that deals "dialectically" with the irrational, with regression into barbarism—that is to say, a strictly negative dialectics. Both Adorno's book of that name and Horkheimer and Adorno's *The Dialectic of Enlightenment*, which traced the "dialectical" descent of reason (in Hegel's sense) into instrumentalism, were little more than mixed farragoes of convoluted neo-Nietzschean verbiage, often brilliant, colorful, and excitingly informative, but often confused, rather dehumanizing and, to speak bluntly, irrational.[24] A "dialectic" that lacks *any* spirit of transcendence *(Aufhebung)* and denies the "negation of the negation" is spurious at its very core.[25] One of the earliest attempts to "dialectically" deal with social regression was the little-known "retrogression thesis," undertaken by Josef Weber, the German Trotskyist theorist who was the exile leader of the Internationale Kommunisten Deutschlands (IKD). Weber authored the IKD's program, "Capitalist Barbarism or Socialism," published in November 1944 in Max Schachtman's *New International* during the bitterest days of the Second World War and posed the question that many thinking revolutionaries of that distant era faced: what forms would capitalism take *if* the proletariat failed to make a socialist revolution after the Second World War?[26] As the title of the IKD document suggests, not all Marxists, perhaps fewer than we may think, regarded socialism as "inevitable" or thought that there would necessarily be a socialist "end to history" after the war. Indeed, many whom I knew as a dissident Trotskyist fifty years ago were convinced that barbarism was as serious a danger for the future as socialism was its greatest hope.27 The prospect of barbarism that we face today may differ in form from what revolutionary Marxists faced two generations ago, but it does not differ in kind. The future of Civilization is still very much in the balance, and the very memory of alternative emancipatory visions to capitalism are becoming dimmer with each generation.

Although the "imaginary" and subjective are certainly elements in social development, contemporary capitalism is steadily dissolving the uniqueness of "imaginaries" of earlier, more diverse cultures. Indeed, capitalism is increasingly leveling and homogenizing society, culturally and economically, to a point that the same commodities, industrial techniques, social institutions, values, even desires, are being "universalized" to an unprecedented degree in humanity's long career. At a time when the mass-manufactured commodity has become a fetish more potent than any archaic fetish that early cultures "imagined"; when the glossy tie and three-piece suit are replacing traditional sarongs, cloaks, and shoulder capes; when the word *business* requires fewer and fewer translations in the world's diverse vocabularies; and when English has become the lingua franca not only of so-called "educated classes" but people in ordinary walks of life (need I add more to this immensely long list?), it is odd that the idiosyncratic in various cultural constellations is now acquiring a significance in academic discourse that it rarely attained in the past. This discourse may be a way of side-stepping a much-needed examination of the challenges posed by recent capitalist developments, and instead mystifying them in convoluted discussions that fill dense academic tomes and, particularly in the case of Foucault and postmodernism, satisfying the "imaginaries" of self-centered individuals, for whom the spray paint can has become the weapon of choice with which to assault the capitalist system and a hairstyle the best way to affront the conventional petty bourgeoisie.

Stated bluntly: no *revolutionary* movement can grow if its theorists essentially deny Bloch's "principle of hope," which the movement so needs for an inspired belief in the future; if it denies universal History that affirms sweeping common problems that have besieged humanity over the ages; if it denies the shared interests that give a movement the basis for a common struggle in achieving a rational dispensation of social affairs; if it denies a processual rationality and a growing idea of the Good based on more than personalistic (or "intersubjective" and "consensual") grounds; if it denies the powerful civilizatory dimensions of social development (ironically, dimensions that are in fact so useful to contemporary nihilists in criticizing humanity's failings); and if it denies historical Progress. Yet in present-day theoretics, a series of events replaces History, cultural relativism replaces Civilization, and a basic pessimism replaces a belief in the possibility of Progress. What is more sinister, mythopoesis replaces reason, and dystopia the prospect of a rational society. What is at stake in all these displacements is an intellectual and practical regression of appalling proportions—an especially alarming development today, when theoretical clarity is of the utmost necessity. What our times require is a *social* analysis that calls for a revolutionary and ultimately popular movement, not a *psycho-analysis* that issues self-righteous disclaimers for "beautiful souls," ideologically dressed in cloaks of personal virtue.

Given the disparity between what rationally *should be* and what currently *exists*, reason may not necessarily become embodied in a free society. If and when the realm of freedom ever does reach its most expansive form, to the extent that we can envision it, and if hierarchy, class, domination, and exploitation were ever abolished, we would be obliged to enter that realm only as *free beings*, as truly rational, ethical, and empathetic "knowing animals," with the highest intellectual insight and ethical probity, not as brutes coerced into it by grim necessity and fear. The riddle of our times is whether today's relativists would have equipped us intellectually and ethically to cross into that most expansive realm of freedom. We cannot merely be *driven* into greater freedom by blind forces that we fail to understand, as Marxists implied, still less by mere *preferences* that have no standing in anything more than an "imaginary," "instincts," or libidinal "desires."[28]

The relativists of our time could actually play a sinister role if they permitted the "imaginative" to loosen our contact with the objective world. For in the absence of rational objective standards of behavior, imagination may be as demonic as it may be liberatory when such standards exist; hence the need for *informed* spontaneity—and an *informed* imagination. The exhilarating events of May-June 1968, with the cry "Imagination to Power!" were followed a few years later by a surge in the popularity of nihilistic postmodernism and poststructuralism in the academy, an unsavory metaphysics of "desire," and an apolitical call for "imagination" nourished by a yearning for "self-realization."

More than ever, I would insist, we must invert Nietzsche's dictum "All facts are interpretations" and demand that all interpretations be rooted in objectivity. We must seek out broader interpretations of socialism than those that cast socialist ideals as a science and strangled its movements in authoritarian institutions. At a time when we teeter between Civilization and barbarism, the current apostles of irrationality in all their varied forms are the chthonic demons of a dark world who have come to life not to explicate humanity's problems but to effect a dispiriting denial of the role of rationality in History and human affairs. My disquiet today lies not in the absence of scientific "guarantees" that a libertarian socialist society will appear—one that, at my age, it will never be my privilege to see—but in *whether it will even be fought for* in so decadent and desperate a period.

—February 15, 1994

NOTES

1. Moreover, despite this tendency to bifurcate objectivity and subjectivity, the two do not exclude each other. There is always a subjective dimension to objectivity, but it is precisely the *relationship* between the two that requires explication.

2. Moral relativism has recently been the breeding ground of a purely functional or instrumental form of rationality, which in my view is one of the greatest impediments to serious social analysis and a meaningful ethics. "Subjective reason," to use Max Horkheimer's phrase from *The Eclipse of Reason*, on which a relativistic approach rests, has been one of the major afflictions of Anglo-American thinking, not merely within the academy but within the general public.

3. Predicated as their self-realization is in their own potentialities, human beings *nevertheless cannot do as they please*, despite the assertions of "beautiful souls," to use Hegel's phrase, who live in an aerie of personal liberation and self-contained "autonomy." Here, Marx was a good deal ahead of today's individualistic anarchists who have a bad habit of disrupting serious attempts at organization and theoretical inquiry with simplistic cries of "Freedom now!"

4. Nothing is easier, more mystifying, and more smug these days than to advance sweeping, ahistorical generalizations about figures like Hegel, Marx, and Lenin. It is evidence of the ugly intellectual degradation of our time that people who should know better make them so flippantly. One might as well claim that Stalin's totalitarianism had its roots in Machiavelli's so-called "Atlantic Republican Tradition" since the latter was the author of *The Prince*; or in Plato, as Karl Popper so notoriously did. Yet Hegel would undoubtedly have resolutely opposed Marx's view of the dialectic; Marx might very well have disowned Lenin, as the Marxist Rosa Luxemburg and the council communists Görter and Pannekoek did; and Stalin would certainly have imprisoned Lenin, as Lenin's widow bitterly reproached Trotsky in 1925, after the former Red Army commander belatedly began to attack Stalin.

5. Many of these former Marxists (particularly "New Left" students and their professors) polluted the sixties with their pet dogmas, only to "grow up" after they had "had their fun" (to rephrase a cynical expression of many Parisian veterans of 1968) and are now polluting the nineties with skepticism, nihilism, and subjectivism. The most serious obstacles to the development of an authentic New Left today are the Alain Touraines, André Gorzes, and Michael Walzers who have rallied variously to "market socialism," "minimal statism," or pluralized concepts of justice

and freedom that are perfectly compatible with modern capitalism. The worst fate that an idea can meet is to be kept artificially alive, long after it has died historically, in the form of graduate courses at the New School for Social Research in New York City.

6. It is easy, when criticizing scientism as an ideology, to forget the role that the natural *sciences* themselves played in subverting beliefs in witchcraft and superstition, and in fostering a secular and naturalistic approach to reality. I would like to think that we no longer believe in Dracula, or in the power of the crucifix to fend off vampires, or in the occult power of women to communicate with demons—or do we?

7. See my "Introduction: A Philosophical Naturalism," elsewhere in this book.

8. Indeed, there may be a "logic to events," but it would be the logic of conventional reason, based on mere cause-and-effect and the principle of identity, *A equals A,* not dialectical reason.

9. See James Miller, *The Passion of Michel Foucault* (New York: Simon & Schuster, 1993).

10. See my forthcoming book *Reenchanting Humanity* (London: Cassell, 1995), for a more detailed discussion of these issues.

11. Ironically, it even vitiates the meaning of *social* anarchism as an ethical socialism.

12. I find no solace in the notion that preliterate peoples "enjoyed" an "affluent society," as Marshall Sahlins would have it. Their lives were all too often short, their cultures burdened by superstition and bereft of a syllabic system of writing, and they normally were at war with each other, to cite only their major afflictions, pastoral New Age images of their lives to the contrary.

13. Indeed, even nominalistic historians who see History as a series of accidents often tacitly presuppose the existence of the "nonaccidental" (perhaps even the *rational*) in a social development.

14. See chapter 11 of my *The Ecology of Freedom* (1982; reprinted by Montreal: Black Rose Books, 1992).

15. I find no view more one-sided and noxious than Theodor Adorno's dictum, "No universal history leads from savagery to humanitarianism, but there is one leading from the slingshot to the megaton bomb." This inflated, less than thought-out pronouncement, taken together with Adorno's commitment to a negativity that rejected sublation (*Aufhebung*), or social and ideological advances, was a step toward nihilism, indeed, an ugly demonization of humanity, that belied his affirmations of reason. See *Negative Dialectics*, trans. E. B. Ashton (New York: Seabury Press, 1973), p. 320.

16. I deliberately eschew the words Totality and *Spirit* to preclude any such suggestion.

17. The name of another chapter in *The Ecology of Freedom*.

18. G.W.F. Hegel, "Reason as Lawgiver," in *Phenomenology of Spirit*, trans. A. V. Miller (Oxford: Oxford University Press, 1977), pp. 252-56.

19. Hegel, for all his entanglements with the notion of *Geist* or "Spirit" and despite his conception of a predetermined "Absolute," at least had the good sense to distinguish the self-development of nonhuman life-forms, for instance, from the self-development of humanity or, for that matter, society. See G.W.F. Hegel, "Introduction," *Lectures on the History of Philosophy*, vol. 1, trans. E. S. Haldane and Frances H. Simson (1892; London: Routledge and Kegan Paul, and New York: The Humanities Press, 1955, 1968), pp. 22-23.

20. Present-day cosmology and biophysics, however, are coming up against phenomena whose explanation requires the flexible concepts of development advanced by dialectical naturalism.

21. Karl Marx, "Toward a Critique of Hegel's Philosophy of Law: Introduction," *Writings of the Young Marx on Philosophy and Society*, trans. Lloyd D. Easton and Kurt H. Guddat (Garden City, N.Y.: Doubleday and Co., 1967), p. 259.

22. W. T. Stace's *Critical History of Greek Philosophy*, for example, shows how a series of ancient Greek thinkers rounded out increasingly full but still one-sided views to produce the most advanced dialectical philosophy of their time, particularly that of Aristotle. Certainly the development of insight into the dialectical nature of reality did not end with the Greeks. Nor will it end with thinkers in our time, any more than science ended in the nineteenth century, when so many physicists thought little more could be added to complete Newtonian physics. In his history of philosophy, Hegel pointed out not only different *degrees* of dialectical reason, which approximated different degrees of truth (which in no way means that he was a "relativist"), but different *kinds* of rationality—"Understanding" or *Verstand*, of the commonsensical kind, and "Reason" or *Vernunft*, of the dialectical kind.

23. Recently, dialectical naturalism has been criticized for committing the "epistemological fallacy," in which a priori concepts become their own conditions of validity, rendering dialectics as such a self-validating system. This, as if dialectic naturalism were not structured around the *reality* of potentiality and were purely an a priori speculative form of reason. Yet these critics themselves usually use the kind of logic that employs the most a priori, indeed tautological of all concepts, the principle of identity, *A equals A*, in preference to dialectical reason.

24. This view is not new for me. In *The Ecology of Freedom*, completed in 1980 and published in 1982, I was at pains to indicate that "the *Dialectic of Enlightenment* is actually no dialectic at all—at least not in its attempt to explain the negation of reason through its own self-development" (p. 272). My respect for the Frankfurt School rested largely on its insightful critique of positivism, which was the dominant philosophical fad in American universities and social theory (so-called "sociology") in the 1940s and 1950s, and on its various insights into Hegelian philosophy. Today, these valuable contributions are far outweighed by the ease with which the Frankfurt School's work has fostered postmodern views in the United States and Germany and by the extent to which its products, especially Adorno's writings, have become academic commodities.

25. Nor does a verbal paradox that contrasts seemingly related but opposing ideas, or colorful expressions of alterity, constitute a dialectic in the sense in which I have discussed it here, however much it seems to resemble formulations in Hegel and the best of Marx. Adorno's provocative endeavors of this kind often turn out to be little more than that —provocations.

26. Presented by the IKD's Auslands Kommitee (Committee Abroad), this huge document long predated *Socialisme ou Barbarie*. The ideas that it advanced, however, are moot today. Extrapolating Hitler's seeming war aims of the early 1940s—to reduce industrialized Western European countries to mere satellites of German capital and to agrarianize and depopulate the East—to the world at large, this theory of imperialism (and barbarism) argued that deindustrialization would be exported to undeveloped countries, and not, as old Marxist theories of imperialism had assumed in the prewar period, capital.

27. Nor did we, by the late 1940s, regard the workers' movement—indeed, "workers' councils" or "workers' control of industry"—as revolutionary, especially with the sequelae of the great strike movements of the late 1940s, which directly affected my own life as a worker.

28. The notion of an "instinct for freedom," touted by many radical theorists, is a sheer oxymoron. The compelling, indeed necessitarian character of instinct makes it the very antithesis of freedom, whose liberating dimensions are grounded in choice and self-consciousness.